Get P|

C000261390

All-Age Services

Nathan Burley,
Julian Milson & Nigel Styles

PT RESOURCES

CHRISTIAN
FOCUS

Copyright © Proclamation Trust

paperback ISBN 978-1-5271-0383-2
epub ISBN 978-1-5271-0431-0
mobi ISBN 978-1-5271-0432-7

10 9 8 7 6 5 4 3 2 1

Published in 2019
by
Christian Focus Publications Ltd.,
Geanies House, Fearn, Ross-shire,
IV20 1TW, Great Britain
with
Proclamation Trust Resources,
Willcox House, 140-148 Borough High Street,
London, SE1 1LB, England, Great Britain.
www.proctrust.org.uk

www.christianfocus.com

Cover design by Tom Barnard

Printed in Malta

CONTENTS

Series Preface

In 1592, the Puritan William Perkins published a tract on preaching that he called 'The Art of Prophesying'. He recognised that 'the preparation of sermons is an everyday task in the church, but it is still a tremendous responsibility and by no means easy. In fact it is doubtful if there is a more difficult challenge in the theological disciplines than that of homiletics .'

Since its beginnings in the summer of 1981, the Proclamation Trust has been committed to helping preachers in that tremendous – and difficult – responsibility. We believe that the Bible is God's written word and that, by the work of the Holy Spirit, as it is faithfully preached, God's voice is truly heard. With Perkins, we are confident that through the preaching of the Word 'those who hear are called into the state of grace, and preserved in it'.

This series of short booklets is designed to help preachers in that 'everyday task'. Experienced practitioners share their wisdom, gained after years of 'toil, struggling with all his energy that he powerfully works within us' (Col. 1:28-29).

We hope that these short booklets will help all of us to progress in our understanding of the task in hand; to set the novice preacher on a course of faithful preaching; to hone the skills of the experienced preacher; to help preaching groups sharpen one another.

However you use this book we hope that it will achieve its twin aims. That you would get preaching (understanding the task at hand), and get preaching (doing more preaching). May

God use these books to renew a commitment in all of us to preach the Word (2 Tim. 4:2).

Jon Gemmell & Nigel Styles
Series Editors

Introduction

This book is about preaching at All-Age Services.

You mean, 'doing the children's talk'?

No. We really do mean preaching. Not swapping the sermon for a Bible-based story. Not a two-minute pause for thought. Proper preaching.

Really?

Yes. At an All-Age Service!

We believe that preaching is for the whole church, not just for adults. Exactly what preaching looks like will change depending on whom we are addressing, but it ought still to be expository preaching, with the Bible at the centre.

Actually, it ought to be an expository service, with the main thrust of the Bible passage shaping everything that takes place, from the welcome at the start to the coffee at the end.

Same as every week.

But with children there too. And OAPs. And teenagers. And babies. And single mums. And ... everyone!

Sound difficult? We agree. That's why we wrote this book. We wrote it for:

- regular preachers who want help adapting to an All-Age setting
- those who normally teach children and young people, but who find themselves needing to plan an entire church service

- church leaders and children's workers who want to include young people in the life of the church without dumbing down
- planning teams who could read it together to spark ideas
- unconvinced church members who need persuading that All-Age Services really are worthwhile

To that end, chapter one aims to help us consider <u>why</u> we ought to do All-Age Services in the first place, letting the Bible shape our motivations for that.

The next couple of chapters deal with <u>how</u> to do it. Chapter two covers how to approach preparing a sermon for an All-Age Service, taking the Bible just as seriously as for any other talk. Chapter three considers how to let the main thrust of the passage affect every aspect of the All-Age Service, not only the talk.

The final section of the book contains examples to help illustrate what we mean. This is the literary equivalent of inviting you along to our churches on an All-Age week to get a feel for what we would do.

Of course, there is a danger that readers might just skip to the end and nick the examples without really understanding the theory! That would be a shame. We are happy for people to pillage any ideas that will help your church. But the best help would be for you to fully grasp what makes a good All-Age Service so that you can come up with even better ideas for yourself. We would be honoured to give you a leg-up.

Obviously, these ideas and examples will need to be translated for your own congregation and refined for the resources that you have available. Some churches have a tradition of children being in 'regular' church services most of the time, which obviously affects what we are saying here. If that is your practise, we greatly respect that and hope that this book might nevertheless be helpful as you think about even these 'normal' services. Each reader may well end up doing All-Age Services very differently to the way we suggest, but we pray that we will still have given you food for thought.

It is our prayer that this book would encourage and challenge you to 'Get Preaching at All-Age Services' ...

A note:

This book has been written by three people. We have worked together, on and off, in various combinations, in different churches, for many years. None of the churches we have worked in have been big churches by any means, and though some of the elements in this book may come across as a bit daunting and unattainable we hope our ideas might spark your ideas, clarify your thinking and be helpful to you as you seek to serve your church family as well as possible.

In writing this book, when we say 'I', we mean that something happened to only one of us; we have avoided being pedantic about which one of us is telling the story.

Everything that you will read in this book comes out of our experience of regularly producing All-Age Services together (and with others). It's all been road-tested (with some improvements after early disasters!). We share the same conviction: All-Age Services are worth doing. We've become persuaded about that. Please let us try to persuade you.

1
Why Bother with All-Age Services?

Let's be honest, when it's an All-Age Service next Sunday, you just want some practical tips. Those are coming later in the book.

First we need to be clear why we have All-Age Services at all. Only when we know why we do them will we be in a position to do them well, and do them with joy.

Here's the big idea: All-Age Services are worth doing because they reflect the true nature of the church.

How? Because they are frequently messy and often a pain? Well yes, that is often true! But more than that, All-Age Services are a way of respecting how God has chosen to set up the church. And helping us to grow into His design.

Church is an all age family

Until we grasp that church is an all age family (whether we like it or not), we will never take All-Age Services seriously. But that is precisely what the church is.

God is not a loner. He is a Trinity – three Persons and yet one God, wonderfully complex and yet utterly united. He created us in His image, so it is not good for us to be loners either. We were built to live in community with Him and with one another. Sin has shattered those relationships. But, through Christ, in the church, God is gathering together again a diverse yet united people.

Time and time again in the Bible, God refers to His people as a family. Salvation is being adopted into this family

(Eph. 1:5). The Father of our Lord Jesus Christ is now <u>our</u> Father (Matt. 6:9). Jesus is not ashamed to call us brothers (Heb. 2:11). Fellow believers are siblings and should treat one another as such (1 Tim. 5:1-2). The testing ground for church leaders is the home because the two are so similar – if someone can't lead his own family, how can he lead the household of God (1 Tim. 3:4-5)?

In short, church is a family.

And this family is made up of all sorts of people. The gospel tears down the barriers that so often separate people in the world. In Christ we are one (Gal. 3:28), both men and women, Jews and Gentiles, rich and poor, slave and free. And even young and old.

It would not be reasonable to say that, while Jew and Gentile Christians are now technically one family, we still don't want to actually meet together! Or that men and women should always go off to separate groups. James specifically calls the rich and poor to mingle (James 2:1-4).

So how could it be acceptable always to push children out of the main gathering of the church? Answer: it's not.

Deuteronomy 31:12-13 speaks of gathering men, women and little ones to hear God's word and learn to fear Him together. Nehemiah 8:1-8, that great picture of the gathered church, calls everyone who can understand what they are hearing to come together and be taught. And then, just in case, people are sent round the assembly to ensure that everybody <u>has</u> understood it! What about those who were unable to understand? If 'everyone' had gathered, then there was nobody left to babysit, so presumably the little ones must have come too!

Time and time again, God's gathered people are a mixed bag of ages. In the book of Acts, whole households worship God together. Paul presumes that children will be present in the

Colossian and Ephesian churches to hear him apply the gospel specifically to them and their parents.

If anything, you would need to make a biblical case that our church gatherings shouldn't be an All-Age Service every week!

There <u>are</u> practical and biblically defensible reasons for teaching people in age-specific settings without denying our unity. But we must be careful what we communicate as we do that. Church is an all age family. We ought to actively cultivate a sense of that within our churches.

Children are not the church of tomorrow – they are part of the church today. It would be strange never to express that by meeting altogether. Or to express it in a way which doesn't acknowledge their presence, their gifts, and their needs. An All-Age Service can't be one that allows children to be there, but makes no allowances for them being there.

All-Age Services aim to make those allowances, both adults for children <u>and</u> children for adults. When we do this, we better express the fact that local church congregations are all age families.

Church is not about me

Another way that All-Age Services reflect the true nature of the church is that they vividly demonstrate that church is not about me. And in case you were in any doubt, church is not about you either.

The more we live out the reality that church is an all age family, the more we are confronted with our own selfishness. Again, God has designed it that way on purpose so that we might help one another to grow. It is not always comfortable and cosy in God's family. Sometimes it is frustrating. All-Age Services are a great opportunity to get over ourselves.

Let's admit it: sometimes All-Age Services are just terrible. Hopefully this book will help fight against some of that.

However, people's problem with All-Age Services is often that they simply don't like how God has designed the church.

Of course, the church is not just a family. It is also a body made up of many different parts (1 Cor. 12:12-27). Which is really annoying because obviously it would be better if it were just made up of people exactly like me! We would rarely say that out loud, but it can be implicit in our criticisms of All-Age Services.

When teenagers despise the interactive parts of the service, they are saying, 'I wish little kids weren't part of the church. They are so embarrassing. Why can't everyone be cool like me?'

When adults look down on shorter talks, they are saying, 'I don't want to be in this family with people like that. Why can't everyone have a long attention span like me?'

When children would rather stay out in their groups, they are saying, 'I would prefer a church which is just targeted at me and my friends without the boring bits. Why can't everyone be fun and entertain me?'

As church leaders and preachers, how much of our frustration with planning and running All-Age Services is actually annoyance at having to bear other people in mind? We would much rather aim things at people like us.

So long as we think church is about me, we won't like it when people unlike us take a full part in things. We will point to the bits we don't like as proof that All-Age Services don't work. The fact that they are hard work will be presented as a reason not to try.

We have heard people call them 'No Age Services', because obviously both adults and children hate them. Aside from being untrue, this is a good point. An All-Age Service is sometimes going to feel like a No Age Service because it is a compromise. It is not a grown-up service with kids sitting in silence. Nor is it a kids' service with grown-ups forced to play along. There ought to be something for everyone. But in practice this means that if any one person liked every bit of it, then we are probably getting it wrong. And conversely, if everybody had a bit they didn't like, we might be on the right track.

Church is not about me and my preferences. All-Age Services highlight this and bring our selfishness to the surface. One way of handling that is to stop doing them. Another is to confront the selfishness and call one another to repent.

A word to adults

Older Christians – generally the more mature Christians – ought to be more selfless and patient. Remember that children are watching you. Please don't roll your eyes or groan. Please don't refuse to join in. Please don't speak badly of these services, especially to children. Please lend a hand to parents who are struggling instead of tut-tutting at them.

Most importantly, please don't harden your heart. It is a dangerous thing to hear God's Word (however it is taught) and tune out. Mature Christians are easily edified. Be humble enough to see that it is good to be reminded of things and to have gospel truth spelt out simply. We ought to take God very seriously. But we ought to take ourselves a lot less seriously.

A word to parents

Please be positive about All-Age Services when talking at home. Some parents resent not being able to cart off 'their darling little brats' to be someone else's problem for an hour! They let their kids know it and everyone else in church pays for it. ('If you're so keen for them to be here, you can entertain them. If not, this is the behaviour you'll get.') That is selfish.

Of course, most parents are not trying to be disruptive like that. They are just desperate for peace and quiet themselves, and are terribly embarrassed to be denying it to others. Nobody's children are perfect and your leaders should make it clear from the front that they expect a bit of fussing and fidgeting.

That said, do please try to keep your children under control. Model full engagement. Whisper encouragements to them to take part and listen. Don't be too quick to whisk them out to the crèche area. Obviously don't distract others by bringing noisy toys with you. But also consider whether the quiet toys you've brought are actually just distracting your own children and teaching them that church doesn't require their full attention.

A word to ministers

If you can teach children, then probably you can teach anyone. Please don't always pass these talks off to the children's worker. You are the pastor of the whole church. It is often pride that makes us unwilling to preach shorter simpler sermons. We need to get over ourselves most of all.

Bend over backwards to preach to the people in the room, not just to your peers. As spiritual fathers, do not exasperate your children, either by giving 45-minute lectures to squirming toddlers, or by giving baby food to adults. The rest of this book aims to help all of us get this right.

A word to children and young people

Please bear with the grown-ups. Not all of the service is for you. Please put up with it. You won't understand it all, but see if there is at least one thing you can take away. The adults would love to chat to you about the one thing you learnt during an All-Age Service.

Your normal groups might be better suited to you. Good. That's why you do those most of the time. But this is good for you too. The full gathering of the church every week is where you are eventually heading. Learn to love praying together, hearing the Bible read and preached, singing in the full congregation. If nothing else, your poor Sunday School teachers are getting a break so going along with it is serving them.

A word to everyone
Remember, everyone. Church is not about me. All-Age Services express this and help us to live it out, bearing with one another in love.

Church is about growing up together
All-Age Services sound like really hard work. They are. As are most things worth doing. We need to be convinced that they are worth the trouble. It is good to put our preferences aside for the sake of others. But only if it actually does them good!

Thankfully, All-Age Services are a genuinely good idea and a brilliant opportunity for everyone to grow together.

All-Age Services help children and young people to grow up
High numbers of children grow up and leave the church. Might one reason be that they were always syphoned off into age-specific groups and never encouraged to see themselves as part of the full congregation? Then they become adults and are expected to feel at home somewhere they have never been before.

All-Age Services are a wonderful stepping-stone into normal church. This is why they must not degenerate into 'children's services'. It is important that they don't differ too extremely from a normal church service. All the elements should be there (prayer, singing, confession, Bible reading, preaching, etc.) but in a way that both stretches younger people and helps them to grow into it. (More on this in chapter 3.)

It is also good for children to hear their parents being taught. Adults are never simply people in authority, but are always under authority too. All-Age Services can model that well. They help younger people to eavesdrop on what is expected of people in the next age bracket up from them.

All-Age Services help adults to grow up

As we have already seen, one way All-Age Services help adults to grow up in maturity is by encouraging them to grow down in humility. But that isn't the only way.

Preaching aimed at All-Ages needs to be even clearer than normal. Points are usually very memorable and refreshingly vivid. That will do all of us good. All-Age Services force preachers to work harder at their explanations, their illustrations, their applications, and their sermon length. Improved preaching benefits everybody, even on a 'normal' week.

Newcomers and unbelievers especially benefit. In the effort to include children, we will state truth more plainly, and this helps adults who wouldn't hear it otherwise or feel too silly to ask what we mean. Christians are sometimes embarrassed to bring their non-Christian friends to All-Age Services for fear of being made to look childish. But new people coming to church often appreciate things being pitched in a clearer and more relaxed way. And anyway, no All-Age Service should ask anything embarrassing or belittling of a visitor (or anyone else).

Many people grew up in homes where the Bible was not opened. Those who were taught well at home probably haven't seen the Bible being taught well to children since they were children themselves. All-Age Services provide an opportunity to model for parents (especially dads) how to engage with the Bible in a way that the whole family can get into. The gathered church can do things on a bigger scale, but there are many things people can pick up about how they might do family devotionals around the breakfast table.

On a similar note, All-Age Services are training opportunities for the usual kids' group leaders, helping them to see how they might better teach the Word faithfully and engagingly to those at a different age and stage to them.

All-Age Services help everyone to grow together

One of the great benefits of All-Age Services is the opportunity to be all together and to enjoy sitting under God's Word as one big family. Far from excluding those without children, they draw everybody in. One of our favourite things in an All-Age Service is to see groups of people (some related, some not) huddled around a Bible together, helping one another to find treasure in God's Word. A moment like that reminds us that none of us are truly 'grown-ups'. We are all 'growing-ups'.

Perhaps 'All-Age' isn't the best name for this. To reclaim a gospel word, they are 'inclusive services', deliberately and self-consciously cultivating a sense of being one body, whatever the differences are which might otherwise divide us. Personally I would stick with 'All-Age' over 'inclusive' so as not to give the impression that our normal services are somehow 'exclusive' rather than welcoming. But any opportunity to lower the entry points to participation is good for the whole congregation.

Conclusion

What we believe about the church shapes what we do when we gather. If deep down we think of church as a deadly serious place for silent and solemn reflection, we will not make space for all ages. If we treat church as a place for me to get my needs met, we will shun anything which pushes us outside our comfort zone. If we see church as just a bit of fun, we will let the kids run riot.

But if church is a family growing together, that will change everything.

We like to think of All-Age Services as being like family mealtimes. Imagine one now. Everyone is laying the table. Lots of wholesome home cooking is being lovingly served out. There's chat and laughter and enjoyment and fun. A lovely atmosphere.

Sometimes the conversation is with and about the children: what was your day like at school? ... try and eat up all that pasta ... would you like a game of Monopoly after tea? And when conversation is like this, the adults all pitch in too.

Sometimes the conversation is between adults. And the children are still at the table, not particularly interested in the things that are being discussed, but still there.

Sometimes the discussion is an all-family activity, planning next summer's holiday or talking about where Granny will sleep when she comes to stay. And the best family mealtimes usually involve an even wider group – the extended family, and some other friends who are joining us for the evening.

Of course, sometimes the adults would prefer a civilised candlelit dinner for two. Sometimes the kids would rather get up and run around. Sometimes the teenagers want to watch TV while they eat. Everyone is going to need to compromise. The adults are going to have to put up with a bit of noise. The children really do need to behave themselves at the table. But it is worth it. The dinner table is about more than just stuffing our faces. Not only are we all being fed, but we are together.

Church is an all age family. It is not about me or you, but about us. It is about God growing us together as a family who worship Him. All-Age Services can be a terrific way to reflect this truth and make it increasingly a reality.

2
TAKING THE BIBLE SERIOUSLY

Having considered <u>why</u> we should do All-Age Services, we are now in a position to think about <u>what</u> we should do in those services and <u>how</u>.

Our plea is simply this: keep the Bible as the main thing in every All-Age Service.

Why the church gathers

Let's do some background digging first. And let's not think explicitly about All-Age Services to start with, but consider why the church gathers at all.

We begin with the Old Testament story of the Exodus. We are told that, before the moment when God brought Israel out of Egypt, He had not made Himself known to them as the Lord (Exod. 6:2-8). This is a strange thing to say because there are occasions in the book of Genesis where the name 'the Lord' <u>is</u> used. For example, straight after the tragic story of Cain, people began to call upon 'the name of the Lord' (Gen. 4:26). And after he was brought safely through water, Noah built an altar 'to the Lord' (Gen. 8:20). But Exodus is telling us that no one in Genesis had yet seen this Lord do the things He now does ... deliver, redeem, take you, bring out, bring in and give you a land. It is only at the Exodus, as He redeems Israel, that God gives this explicit content to that four-letter name 'Lord'. He is now to be known by all Israel (Exod. 6:6-7), by all Egypt (7:5), by all the world (9:16), for all time (3:15) as the One who 'brought you out of the land of Egypt' (20:2). The Redeemer.

But the book of Exodus doesn't end once the rescue is completed at chapter 15. It continues until after the almost-interminable chapters 25-40 concerned with the construction of the tabernacle. Exodus 29:46 is a key verse. God 'brought them out of the land of Egypt ... *that I might dwell with them.*' God will bring them <u>out</u> of Egypt, and <u>to</u> a land of blessing and prosperity for sure (Exod. 3:8). But the purpose of God's rescue is <u>first</u> to bring God's people to God Himself.

Exodus 19 tells the story of what happens when God's people are brought to God Himself. It is scary! It happens at a mountain that is all smoke, fire, noise and earthquake. 'No entry' signs circle it so that the mass of people must remain outside crash-barrier limits, only seventy elders may 'come up' and worship God from afar, and then only solo Moses may 'come near'. This mountain advertises a simple truth: when they are brought to God Himself, God's people can come near but they also can't come near!

This gathering in Exodus 19 is 'church'. That's the word Stephen uses to describe it in Acts 7:38 (where the word is usually translated 'congregation' or 'assembly'). And what marks this assembly, according to Exodus and Deuteronomy, is the voice of God. God's people gather to hear.

The thing is, of course, that the voice of this speaking God that they gather to hear is very scary too. The people beg with Moses, 'you speak to us, and we will listen; but do not let God speak to us, lest we die' (Exod. 20:19). So 'the people stood far off, while Moses drew near to the thick darkness where God was'. And then subsequently, he 'came and told the people all the words of the Lord' (Exod. 24:3). You'll need to read this next sentence several times: the point of the scariness is not so that Israel will be afraid, but so that she will be afraid (Exod. 20:20)! Or to explain: they are not to fear that this scary scene means that God will destroy them here and now ... for

He will not. But they <u>are</u> to fear Him in such a way that it leads to their obedience to whatever He says.

Deuteronomy 4 looks back at this scene with 40 years hindsight. In case we missed the point, it is now made very clear. When 'the Lord spoke to you out of the midst of the fire, you heard the sound of word, but saw no form; there was only a voice' (4:12). Central to any meeting with the true God is not 'a form' but 'a word'. The essence of the gathering of God's people is 'listening' not 'seeing'. The people of God gather to hear.

Hebrews 12:18-29 interprets this scene for us as New Testament believers. There is a big contrast between this Exodus 19 Sinai mountain (untouchable, fire, darkness, gloom, tempest, trumpet and terrifying voice) and the heavenly mountain that Christians now approach. We 'come to' the real thing, where God actually is. The writer is broadcasting the superiority of the finished work of Jesus over the inferior Judaism: how much better is the mountain we come to than the mountain of Exodus 19!

Despite this huge contrast, two things remain the same. The first is that God is just as scary: He is still the 'consuming fire', whose earth-shaking power has not diminished and who it is even worse to ignore. The second thing that remains the same is that God is still speaking, and we must not refuse Him. This goes right back to the start of Hebrews where God is speaking 'by his Son' (1:1-4). We must 'pay much closer attention to what we have heard' – that is, to Jesus (2:1-4), and 'not harden our hearts' (3:7-4:13) to what God says to us. We need to do that 'Today' – in other words, every day on which God speaks Jesus to us.

What does this mean for our Christian gatherings? Here's the point. The church still gathers to hear. The essence of our meeting is to be 'word' not 'form'. Obedience to what God says matters infinitely more than running after sensory experience.

Now perhaps you can see why this might be important for All-Age Services. Whatever visual gimmicks we may employ (and as this book goes on, you will discover that we <u>love</u> visual gimmicks!), they must not dilute the central purpose of our gathering: to hear what God says. 'Form' must not compete with, distract from, overwhelm, or drown out 'word'. Everything must serve listening. For, of course, we are listening to the scary God Himself. Every time.

That's why the ascended Christ gives Word-ministers to His church: 'apostles, prophets, evangelists and pastor-teachers' (Eph. 4:11). He gifts His church with Word-proclaimers because the church needs the Word, and needs to listen to the Word. For we were born again 'through this living and abiding Word of God', and we will 'grow up into salvation' by the same pure spiritual milk (1 Pet. 1:23-2:3). It is this Word that 'makes you wise for salvation' and which is to be used 'for teaching, for reproof, for correction, and for training in righteousness' (2 Tim. 3:14-4:5). It gets a whole lot of different names in the surrounding verses in 2 Timothy: 'the sacred writings' (3:15), 'Scripture' (3:16), 'sound or healthy teaching' (4:3), 'the truth' (4:4), but the overall point is clear: the Word will do the work, and grow the church.

That's why the pastor's job is to 'preach the Word' (2 Tim. 4:2) for that is how he will 'reprove, rebuke, exhort'. His job is to speak into any and every situation, not his own bright ideas, but the Word of God. His authority comes from the Word and not from his job title. And as he preaches God's Word, as an under-shepherd, God Himself will be shepherding His flock. The sheep 'know the voice' of their true, good shepherd and 'will listen to that voice' (John 10:4, 16).

When the local church gathers, we gather to hear. We listen to God's word to us. It is the task of the church leader to ensure that the local church congregation can and does hear that Word. And that is to be the characteristic of every church gathering (including every All-Age Service).

How will that happen?

How the church hears

When the pastor-teacher brings the Word of God to a local church congregation, he teaches them and pastors them.

Of course there are many ways in which he can do that.

Simply reading the Bible is the most obvious way. And perhaps we've all had that experience when the straightforward out-loud reading of a Bible passage brings out the meaning in such a way that it is 'nearly preaching'. A well-led small group Bible study is another way of closely listening to the taught word of God. So too is a one-to-one discipling meeting, with the Bible-open. And so too, of course, is the Sunday sermon.

Any one of those 'forms' can (to a greater or lesser extent) be 'expository'. Exposition is simply making clear what God says.

Expository preaching, in David Helm's definition, 'submits the shape and emphasis of the sermon to the shape and emphasis of the biblical text' (*Expositional Preaching,* Crossway, 2014). So 'exposition' refers to the content of the sermon, to the biblical truth that is its subject: 'to bring out of Scripture what is there, and not to thrust in what I think might be there' (Quoted from H.C. Moule, *Charles Simeon,* London: Metahaven & Co., 1892, p. 97).

This is important as many today confuse what we're talking about with a certain style of sermon, which is effectively a running 'oral commentary'. A sermon like this might begin with an introductory amusing story, followed by three points each with an alliterative heading and then end with some applications. But that style of sermon is not necessarily expository preaching.

Even more emphatically, expository preaching is not a lecture where notes are transferred from the preacher's piece of paper to the listener's piece of paper (with no engagement of brain en route). That is no more than a very elementary form of photocopying! There may be lots of quite dull preaching like that, often with far too much material only just squeezed into the time limit, and it may even describe itself as 'expository preaching', but that is not its essence.

Nor is it some Western/European style of public speaking. Each year at the Cornhill Training Course, we have a number of international students who are in the UK to receive our training for just a year or two. I keep telling them not to emulate whatever they perceive to be the <u>style</u> of the preaching they are hearing in the UK. We run regular seminars to help them work out how to apply the principles they are being taught in the very different culture of their homeland. Don't start preaching Westernised sermons: 'be expository' <u>and</u> 'be African' or 'be Malaysian' or 'be Iranian'!

And nor does 'expository preaching' have to be 'sequential preaching'. Many expository preachers do indeed preach all the way through a Bible book over several weeks, and the subject for next Sunday's sermon is always 'the next bit'. There are lots of good reasons why sequential preaching is a good model, and some of those reasons are similar to the reasons for expository preaching ... but these two things are not the same thing.

A sermon can be expository (or not) whether it's on a single verse or a longer passage. It makes no difference whether it lasts five minutes or 45 minutes. And the aim of the speaker is the same whether the 'preaching' is being done at a toddler group, or in a sermon to an adult congregation. It is not determined by the audience. Even a 'topical sermon' can be done in an expository way (though this is difficult in practice, as it requires careful selection of text, a broad and balanced grasp of what else the Bible says on that topic, and an ability to synthesise the whole).

Now here is the main point ... the church pastor is to bring the Word of the Lord to his congregation. They gather to hear that Word. Expository preaching is the best, normal way to pastor the church who gather to hear. For then the Bible text determines every part of the content, every pastoral intention of the preacher, and every application to the congregation. It is God speaking today in a way that is recognisably how He originally spoke these things. If God were in the congregation, listening to this sermon (forgive this very inappropriate picture), I want Him to be nodding along to everything He hears: 'yes, that's exactly what I meant'. And I want that because — and here's a definition as old as Augustine — God speaks when the Bible speaks.

So ... do expository preaching at All-Age Services

By which we mean: let the Bible control everything that is said at every All-Age Service. For the church (and on this particular week, it's the church made up of a whole range of different ages) is gathering to hear. So, make clear what God says. Keep the Bible as the main thing.

Many churches run All-Age Services. Many of them will interrupt their normal series for 'a special, one-off' All-Age talk. It may be both that the children break with their series from Acts, and the adults with their sermons in Amos ... because there is an unspoken assumption that there are 'bits of the Bible that are more appropriate for All-Age Services'.

It's not an easy thing to decide whether the All-Age Service should follow the same series as the 'in church' sermon series or the 'kids groups' material (and often that will still beg the question whether we follow the curriculum of the 5–7s, or the 7-11s, or the 11-14s etc!). We would generally opt for following the adult series, as it is then modelling to adults – and to fathers in particular – how to teach to their family what they themselves are learning from the Bible. But you can make the case either way.

The main thing we would want to query is the idea that there is some kind of 'All-Age Services Bible Curriculum' to which we should turn. Usually this curriculum features Jesus' parables, and some well-known incidents from a Children's Story Bible. The irony is that these are often the trickier passages for children! Jesus told the parables not because they are particularly easy to understand but because they are more difficult to understand (cf. Mark 4:10-13, 33-34): they need additional explanation.

Similarly, many of the so called 'children's stories' aren't as child-friendly as we might think. Noah's Ark? 'I guess you think you know this story. You don't. The real one's much more gory' (as Roald Dahl introduces his retelling of Cinderella in *Revolting Rhymes*). Would you normally tell such a story of devastating human destruction to under-5s? And market it with all manner of tie-in merchandise? There's a reason why the movie *Titanic* has a 15-certificate! Similarly, Daniel in the Lion's Den. Even though you can find online suggestions for 'lion pillow craft' (!), I'm not sure that families being torn to pieces by ravenous wild beasts (Dan. 6:24) is the best bedtime story for an imaginative little-un!

That said, let us overstate our case: there is no bit of the Bible that is not suitable for an All-Age Service. The Bible is a book for all ages. For families. For parents to teach their children. For all social classes. For all levels of education.

Now the caveat. Of course, there are some stories where the content is more 'adult'. For example, if you were preaching through Judges and the division of passages meant that chapter 19 fell on All-Age Week you might want to tweak the programme slightly. That said, with care and discretion, even a chapter like Judges 19 could be taught to all ages.

The worst All-Age talk I ever heard was from Luke 7:36-50. It told the story of the contrast between Simon and the woman. Or, to use his alliterative headings: the story of the Pharisee and the prostitute. Actually, Luke doesn't say that the woman was a prostitute ... but the preacher now had to explain: 'Children, some of you may not know what a prostitute is. It's someone who sells her body for sex. Anyway ...' (That's quite apart from the fact that 'Pharisee' and 'Prostitute' don't actually alliterate!). The end of the talk was 'do you want to be a Pharisee or a prostitute for Jesus?' Gulp! Some of the children present were clearly there without any adult member of their family, and I dread to think what kind of conversation there may have been over the Sunday lunch table. 'What did you learn at church this morning?' 'I want to be a prostitute for Jesus.' Shocked gasps. 'Do you know what a prostitute is?' 'Oh yes, it's someone who sells their body for sex.'

I don't think the preacher needed to dig himself such a deep hole in Luke 7! But it may be that some parts of the Bible concern material that is 'less suitable for younger viewers'. But those parts are fewer and further between than we might imagine. The many examples in this book show that we are willing to have a go at any part of the Bible, and any kind of Bible literature. In our experience, it is always hard to do the Bible preparatory work, and it is always hard to produce good content for a successful All-Age Service ... and that applies whichever bit of the Bible you're looking at.

The big point is: do expository preaching. There is no bit of the Bible that is not suitable for an All-Age Service (– that's the overstating once again!). Just open the Bible and let the Bible speak.

How the preacher prepares

Preparing to preach the Bible at an All-Age Service is the same as preparing for any opportunity to teach the Bible. It's the same as preparing a sermon ... or preparing a 90-minute session for 11–14 year-olds ... or a Bible story for Toddler Group. The steps in understanding any passage so that I teach it correctly are the same all the way through the process.

The only difference comes towards the end of the preparation process when I start to think about how I will teach this. If it is for a small group Bible study, then I need a list of questions to ask my group. If it is next Sunday's sermon then I need whatever written notes I would normally take into the pulpit. If it is a 90-minute session for 11–14 year olds, it would include games, quizzes, crafts, discussion time, up-front Bible teaching, etc.

But before I get to that presentation 'output' stage, I need to work hard at the Bible 'input' stage. No matter what form my teaching will eventually take, I will begin by going through the same steps. I will work at my Bible.

There are lots of books to help the Bible student get to the heart of a Bible passage; to listen to the content in front of us so that we can have confidence we have heard what God wanted to be heard. Some of those resources are provided in other books in this series. I have found that three essential questions to ask of any passage (and to ask in this order) are:

1 What does it say?

This first question is an observation question. We joke at Cornhill that, in the first year of the course, we simply aim to teach our students to read. Just to look and look and look until we see what is in front of us on the page. An important step in that process is learning to put aside all the assumptions that we carry with us as we come to a passage (fragments of past Bible studies, sermons, personal Bible readings ... plus our own general understanding of 'what we think the Bible says'). There is no shortcut to this. Be like a forensic scientist, studying hard at what is actually in front of us.

2 Why does it say this?

This second question helps us to think about the purpose of this verse/passage/chapter. When the original author wrote this, what was he hoping would be the thing that his readers would think or do because they had read it? Or even more significantly, what was he praying for his readers? At Cornhill, we've come to describe this as the 'pastoral intention'. It is something that is thoroughly in line with the purpose of the whole book from which my passage comes.

3 What are the implications?

The third question is about 'application', but 'implications' is a better word. 'Application' suggests 'doing' things, but of course the Bible might lead me to change my 'thinking' first, and 'implications' more easily includes my attitudes as a first arena for change. The point is: God's Word always <u>does</u> things, accomplishing what God intends (Isa. 55:8-11), so we are committed to the theological necessity of change as we gather to hear. What change might this passage imply?

The point of these three questions is simply to aid good understanding. And the point of understanding is to be clear what we are gathering as a church to hear: what does God say? What is His word to us today from what He said to those people then? Study your passage until you are clear what God is saying to us … and then you are ready to crystallise that into your Big Idea.

Teach the Big Idea of the passage

Having completed this initial study work on your passage, summarise the main theme of the passage into a short sentence of 10-12 words. This is the Big Idea of the passage. There's no magic about that phrase 'the Big Idea'. It's just summarising as simply as possible 'the main thing this passage is about'. Or to be theologically more accurate: 'the truth that God is preaching in this Bible passage'. It's emphatically <u>not</u> 'what subject does this passage generally touch on that I'd like to be the main point in my preaching?' Expository preaching is constrained by what this passage <u>exactly</u> says.

Haddon Robinson (in *Expository Preaching* IVP, 1986) explains that it is not only helpful but also necessary for a sermon to centre on one specific thing, a central idea. This idea, he suggests, needs both a subject (i.e. the thing I am talking about) and its complement (i.e. what I am saying about the thing that I am talking about). That's why it's always best that any Big Idea has a verb in it.

For example, a subject for Mark 2:1-12 might be 'the forgiveness of sins' or 'the authority of Jesus'. But until we add its complement, we do not know what we're being told about 'the forgiveness of sins' (and that phrase could equally be the 'subject' for Col. 2:13-14) or 'the authority of Jesus' (which would also fit as the general subject of Mark 2:22 or 5:35-43). So a Big Idea for Mark 2:1-12 might be: Jesus shows His authority to forgive sins by healing the paralytic.

Once the Big Idea is decided, the 'input' stage is complete. It is time to move on to the 'output' stage. And the output we are thinking about in this book is an All-Age Service – not just its 'talk' or sermon, but every part of the service. The next chapter continues this process.

3
ORGANISING AN ALL-AGE SERVICE

By this stage in the proceedings, we are clear on <u>why</u> we have All-Age Services (ch. 1). We have also begun considering <u>how</u> to run them, beginning with taking the Bible seriously (ch. 2). We have worked hard at the passage and we have our Big Idea.

Now what?

In this chapter we're going to consider how to turn that Big Idea into a fully-fledged successful All-Age Service.

Success isn't always easy to identify but, with an All-Age Service, success can be gauged with one very simple question: are we keeping the Bible the 'main thing'?

Some of the most apparently 'successful' All-Age Services fall down on this question because some other element in the service overwhelms the Big Idea of the Bible passage. After the service members of the church family might come up to you and say, 'Great service this morning!' and all they will take away is the image of the pastor filling his face with chocolate cake or trampolining throughout the talk!

Our aim is that everyone leaves with the Big Idea of the Bible passage ringing in their ears. That means that they have clearly heard God speak, and that equates to success. Every part of the process of planning, running and evaluating All-Age Services needs to be tied together by keeping the Word of God at the centre. That may sound like an evangelical cliché, but it is all too easy to run with a good idea rather than run with the Bible.

The rest of this chapter will help us to keep the Bible the main thing.

Planning to plan All-Age Services

If you're not already running All-Age Services, the first question is: 'how often will we have one?' As we've already said, you could make a case for having a weekly All-Age Service but, given that they can be fairly resource-intensive, it may be best to begin with one every quarter and build from there to something like monthly.

Let's assume you have a monthly All-Age Service. The next thing to consider is where it fits in the teaching programme. Is there a separate curriculum for the All-Age Services (so that the regular sermon series is put on hold once each month)? Or do we follow the adult sermon series, or the children's groups curriculum? (There is more on this discussion on pages 27-28.)

All-Age Services can require a lot of resources. As a church you need to plan to dedicate those resources in order to run successful services. Without the appropriate investment of time and people, your All-Age Services will most likely end up being a cringey version of a normal Sunday Service. A church of any size can run All-Age Services, but you need to be realistic about the resource cost and commit to meeting that cost, possibly at the expense of other things you're doing as a church.

One resource you will almost certainly need, is a team to plan individual All-Age Services. It needn't be a huge team with a representative from every age group in your church, although a spread of ages is desirable. The most important consideration is that the team is creative and works effectively together. It will be responsible for producing a clear and achievable plan for the next All-Age Service, which in turn could additionally involve others from the church family in a practical way. People within the team principally need to generate ideas in a creative and practical way that will ensure the Bible is taught well.

An absolute must is that the person who will be giving the talk will be part of this team. They will need to have done much of the work on the passage in advance of the meeting. That way, they can take the lead in keeping the Bible central and steering people back to what needs to be taught. They have power of veto! If an idea is generally true but isn't really going with the thrust of the passage, it's their job to bring things back on track. If the service is to be led by a different person, they need to be at this meeting too.

A team like this presents a great opportunity to train people in how to handle the word of God well. It doesn't need to be made up of theologians – just people with a servant heart who are eager to sit under the authority of Scripture.

The frequency of services, where they fit in your teaching programme and the allocation of resources are part of your wider planning for church life.

We're now going to focus in on the nitty-gritty of actually putting an All-Age Service together.

Putting an All-Age Service together

Your planning team will likely need to meet each month, well in advance of the next All-Age Service. We have found that it works best if the meeting to plan next month's service is in the week immediately after this month's. That will allow maximum time for preparation.

The single most important requirement for this meeting is that the person who will be giving the talk at next month's All-Age Service has done the hard work of understanding the passage that the service will teach. The ideal may be for the All-Age Service planning team to meet for a Bible Study on the passage before they then meet to plan the service, but in most settings that's not a realistic expectation. At the very least, team members should have read the passage a few times before the meeting in order to familiarize themselves with what will be taught.

Then at the planning meeting, after prayer together, the preacher leads a 10-minute mini Bible study to explain how he arrived at the Big Idea of the Bible passage. This is the point to set the direction of the service plan by getting everyone clear on the Big Idea of the passage: this is what we want to teach.

At this point, 'the Big Idea' now needs to suggest 'the Big Image'. Sometimes we've called this 'the gimmick'! We're talking about the controlling metaphor that is suggested by the Big Idea that will be a very clear way of teaching the Big Idea in a way that is immediately understandable, and will prove to be memorable. The Big Image must be under control. We've found that it is easy at this point to get carried away with creatively ludicrous thoughts! Keep asking: what is the image that this idea focuses on?

It may be that the preacher comes to the planning team meeting with both the Big Idea and the Big Image. Or it can be that the planning group work on this together. Either way, it is absolutely crucial that the Big Idea determines the Big Image. If there is any lack of clarity about the Big Idea, then the planning meeting will be derailed as everyone searches for a Big Image without understanding the Big Idea of the passage: the Image will be in the driving seat rather than the Bible.

The Big Image will serve as the principle motif in the service. The search for this image is where the rule, 'no idea is a bad idea' needs to apply. (Of course, it may be that 'bad' ideas are suggested but you don't want to stifle creativity at this point!)

The Big Image may well be suggested in the passage itself. For example, an All-Age Service on 1 Peter 2:9-10 might use the Big Image of 'light and dark'. Or the Big Image may be alluded to in the way that the Big Idea is phrased. For example, the Big Idea of Mark 2:1-12 (on page 32) might suggest something about showing or demonstrating something that is otherwise hidden. You need an open conversation where anything goes and no proposal is too big, too silly, too weird, too messy, too crazy etc. as you hone in on the right image to carry the teaching.

Let's turn to an actual Bible passage for an example. This was part of a two-term series going through Romans in the adult sermons. The passage for next month's All-Age Service is Romans 8:28-30. The conversation at the planning team meeting might go something like this:

> **Preacher**: OK. The Big Idea I've arrived at is this: God is at work through all the ups and downs of life to bring you to glory. (*He then explains his thinking*). So, what should our Big Image be?
>
> **Rick**: Well, there are lots of things linked together in these verses. We could do something with an enormous chain?
>
> **Sue**: A daisy chain? Or what about a paper chain? We could put key words on the bits of paper we link together ... and decorate them!
>
> **Preacher**: Well ... there is a chain in the passage, but that's not really the Big Idea. Could we have something to do with the ups and downs of life?
>
> **Rick**: What about doing the whole service as a sort of News programme? With happy news stories and sad news stories?
>
> **Alison**: We could use the ITV News at Ten theme tune!
>
> **Sue**: Or, we could play a game of Snakes and Ladders? ... A <u>giant</u> game of Snakes and Ladders!
>
> **Nicholas (a pragmatist)**: We'd have to make sure we're covered for Health and Safety if we're working at height ... and if we're handling snakes!

Fun meeting, eh? I hope you get the idea. It may take some work to settle on a Big Image that works well, but it is time well spent. It could be the case that the Big Image only appears during the talk, but the aim is that this image infuses the whole of the service.

In fact, this planning team meeting did end up producing a huge Snakes and Ladders board (roughly 7m square), painted in very bright colours, that filled the floor in the middle of the congregation, who were (unusually) seated on all four sides of it.

This service on Romans 8:28-30 might well become known as the Snakes and Ladders service in the history of the church in which it was done – but of course, it's far more important that people understand <u>why</u> the Snakes and Ladders image was used. And that needs reinforcing throughout the service.

With a Big Idea and Big Image agreed upon, it's time to think about the overall shape of the service and some ideas to potentially include with the talk. Something I've found helpful is to have a planning sheet to aid the process. Below is an example of the kind of thing that might work (see large scale version on page 138):

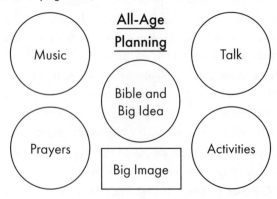

Avoid making the All-Age Service so different that it loses any sense of continuity with other Sundays. A sense of disconnect from other Sundays will mean that people put the All-Age Service into an entirely different category from the usual pattern of services in your church. It will just seem quirky. Keep most, if not all, of the main elements that you'd usually include in all your services. Depending on your church tradition, the All-Age Service might therefore (usually) include a prayer of confession, general prayers, Bible readings, a creed, a talk, the songs you usually sing, communion, notices, interviews or anything else that is part of your usual Sunday time together.

Format your planning sheet (from page 38) to reflect your own situation and practice. Go through the elements you want to include and think about how they can best be used to support your Big Idea, ideally using the vehicle of your Big Image. Once agreed, jot your ideas under the appropriate heading on the planning sheet.

In the example from Romans 8, we decided that as an activity we would ask people to write on Post-it notes either something good that happened to them (to stick it at the bottom of a ladder) or something bad that happened (to stick it at the top of a snake on our giant game board). This would be written under the 'Activities' heading on the planning template above. 'Activities' might well be an element that isn't usually part of your Sunday gatherings. They're good to include in All-Age Services as they increase everyone's involvement and provide 'down-time' for people to chat and families to 're-set', and for different ages to mix in ways that might not normally happen.

Another thing you can include in the activities section is something you could do with the pre-school children in the service. A vibrant and visually stimulating service may well be enough to keep them meaningfully engaged but you might need to think about providing some kind of practical activity that they could quietly do with a parent or in a little group, based on the Big Idea of course, at any point during the service. We have sometimes provided 'All-Age Service Bags' (– just a simple cloth draw-string bag will suffice), colour-coded for different ages. Each month, different items are included that provide activities to reinforce the Big Idea. It's a good idea to give them a base so that parents can support their young children and be part of what's going on in the rest of the service. This is a helpful encouragement to those with young families who may find All-Age Services stressful.

Back to Romans 8. Later on in that service, after the talk, we used the Post-it notes for our prayer time. We prayed for those who had experienced 'the bad' and praised God for the joy of the 'the good' but, having looked at what the Bible had to say about God's purposes for our lives, we were able to thank God for the good and the bad times alike. That, of course, went under the 'Prayer' heading on our planning sheet. Discuss in your team ideas of how to link the prayer time into the Big Idea so that the prayers are an integral part of the whole service rather than simply being an add-on.

You might want to think about different ways you can include your Bible reading(s) too. You could do a dramatic reading, with people who have rehearsed acting out the passage. You could have a mini Bible Study in small groups where people are sitting. Sometimes a word-search, or crossword, or quiz (on a printed service sheet) can be a different way to get small groups interacting with the Bible. You could alternate reading verses between two halves of the church family. You could read the passage with images showing on a screen. You could even just read it! Obviously, read it well!

As the team discusses possible things to include in the Service, some of those ideas may be taken up by the preacher to include with his talk. In our Romans example, the Post-it note activity could have happened at any point in the service before the talk or during the talk itself. You'll need to make a judgement call on the service shape that works best but any good idea that is introduced or used during the talk will have a higher profile in the service. It will stress the link between the Big Idea and the Big Image: we're not just doing this because it's fun, but because it comes straight out of the Bible passage.

As the team discusses music choices, include songs that reinforce the Big Idea. Think too about a range of styles of music, to help encourage and engage all ages. This will mean that you will probably include both 19th-century hymns and modern 'action songs'. Whilst these may well be part of the normal Sunday diet, you'll need to take special care in how the service leader introduces every song in an All-Age Service. With hymns, for example, pick out one or two of the trickier words or concepts in order for everyone to understand, briefly and simply explaining them. Note the 'simply' here. The explanation could potentially become more confusing than what's being explained! With 'action songs,' empathise with those for whom joining in with actions roughly equates to their recurring nightmare of suddenly finding themselves naked in a public place. A simple, 'If you'd like to join in with the actions, this is how they go' will normally suffice.

Now for a checking question to ensure that the Bible really is at the centre of every part of the service: 'how does this reinforce the Bible teaching?' If it doesn't serve that purpose, then reject the idea. If you begin to let things sneak into the service just because they are 'fun' items linked to the Big Image but with no real sense of the Big Idea, then your service will eventually cease to be an All-Age Service and will instead become a free-for-all of messy ideas where the gimmick is king rather than the Bible. Remember that we gather to hear what God says: make sure we listen!

As you plan the various elements of your service, it might be useful to have the following in mind:

- Keep things **accessible**. This means that any bit of the service is easy to join in, and not difficult to watch from the side-lines. It means that there is lots of variety (to cater for different people and different ages). It means that it is very clear why we are doing everything in the service – whether it is something conventional, or something more bizarre! More importantly, keeping things accessible lovingly serves all the members of the church family.

- Keep things **short**. A good rule of thumb is that an All-Age Service should last less than an hour and probably closer to fifty minutes. And it would be unusual for any individual item (other than the talk) to be longer than 4 or 5 minutes.

- Keep things **engaging**. As we've already seen in Chapter 1, each member of our church family has different preferences and will find themselves more attracted to some elements of the service than others. An All-Age Service is of course a great opportunity to better meet the needs of those in our church families who have a different learning style, whatever their age. Whatever we're doing, the item itself should not in and of itself provide the excuse for anyone to disengage: even if their involvement is just watching, we want them to be just as engaged.

Preparing the talk for an All-Age Service

The talk will be the focus of any All-Age Service and whilst the process of writing the talk is very similar to the process you would use to prepare any Bible talk, there are some key differences when preparing a talk for all ages.

Here are some brief pointers to help with the process ... and hopefully the outcome!

Format

The talk for an All-Age Service isn't just a 'normal' sermon using 'simple' words. Of course it <u>should</u> use simple words. But so should every 'normal' sermon!

Often an All-Age Service lends itself to playing with the format of the talk. It can often feel more free-flowing. And, with greater congregational participation, may require more to be 'off the cuff'. I have often preached at an All-Age Service with a very different style of notes in my hand (using index cards rather than a full script). I've sometimes stuck them to the 'props' I'm using in the talk. I've even projected my sermon notes onto the back wall of the church building (behind everyone so they are not distracted), and so been able to preach with nothing in my hand.

Sometimes it might work best to split your talk and place another element or two between the two halves. This element might be a response to what you've all just learnt together. For example, singing a song to help you reflect on the teaching, or a group activity to reinforce the point. However, don't simply split a talk into chunks just to make a long talk seem shorter ... that's cheating!

Very often, the Big Image will help to shape the talk and provide the central illustration to communicate your Big Idea. Sometimes the Big Image will involve the use of props (as in our Snakes and Ladders game above) and will also often involve participation from the church family – sometimes rehearsed, sometimes impromptu.

Be disciplined in keeping the same rules for any aspect of the service: keep it accessible, keep it short and keep it engaging.

Clarity

Be ruthless in making your talk have one point only. And teach that Big Idea. Keep pushing it home. With a normal sermon you might take a detour, or you might refer to other passages at some length but be wary of doing those things in an All-Age talk. Avoid information overload. Your aim is to encourage <u>everyone</u> to leave the service knowing the Big Idea – they've heard it and they've understood it and they've responded to it and they've begun to apply it.

Be clear in the language you use. You need to be understood by the whole church family. You will need to work hard at simplifying your vocabulary and taking the time to explain key concepts that might be unfamiliar to some of those present. This doesn't mean that you dumb down the message; you just have to work hard to explain it with simple words and concepts. Never speak in a patronising way to certain groups. Aim for maximal accessibility.

Length

In our experience, ten to twelve minutes is a good target length for your All-Age talk. This doesn't give you long to teach your Big Idea but it is enough time, especially if every other element of the service is properly focussed too. One of the easiest ways to overshoot on time is to plan the structure of your sermon as you would for any other Sunday, for example, with three main points, the only difference being that in All-Age week you disguise those three points as one!

The general rule is 'teach one point well.' This is not to say that you can't have an All-Age talk with two or more points if the passage you're teaching demands it. But let those two or more points serve the single Big Idea. That said, it may be that you need to tweak the length of your passage if you really are struggling to distil the teaching to one simple Big Idea.

Visuals

Include carefully chosen visuals during the talk in order to ensure it is as accessible as possible for all ages and abilities. If you have the facilities to use a large screen in your church, make good use of it at this service. Providing a variety of modes of communication is a kindness to those who may find it difficult to simply sit and listen. In fact, once I had started to do that in All-Age Services it wasn't long before I continued to do so in every service, trying harder to include everyone who was there.

In general terms, a three-dimensional object is <u>always</u> preferable to a two-dimensional image of it. If you're talking about jelly, use jelly rather than a photo of jelly. If it's a Snakes and Ladders board, create a huge one to cover the floor. Or use a real ladder, and a real snake (... well maybe not!).

Illustrations

In an All-Age talk your illustrations need to be genuinely All-Age. They need to be accessible to all and helpful to all in helping everyone to engage with the Big Idea. To that end, visual illustrations work very well.

Back to our Romans 8 example, the progressive nature of the 'golden chain' in verses 29-30 was illustrated by literally climbing up a step-ladder with each rung representing the activity of God in salvation. The first rung was 'foreknown', the next was labeled 'predestined', then 'called', then 'justified', with 'glorified' at the top.

Remember that you might need to throw in a couple of illustrations of the same point directed at the different generations in the service. So, for example, an illustration that used the 1970s character Mr Benn may need careful explanation to younger people or (better) an additional illustration relevant to them or (best of all) find another illustration that works across the generations today!

Application

Often just a sentence or two applying the Bible passage to various groups will suffice. But sometimes it's even better to be more specific in application and direct different applications to different groups in a more sustained way.

An example of this might be to say to the children: 'It would be great to listen to what I'm about to say to the adults very carefully because one day you'll be adults!'. Or even 'children, I'm just going to say something to the adults for a moment ...'

And equally you might need to say to the adults: 'I don't know how good your memories are, but do you remember what it was like to be 10 years old? As I talk to them for a moment now, why don't you plan to share after the service with one of them how you coped with this aspect of godliness when you were their age.'

You get the idea? It's good to direct what you say to specific groups, but also think of ways in which you can help ensure the continued engagement of everyone else.

Evaluating your All-Age Service

Start each planning team meeting with a review of the last All-Age Service. Don't miss this vital self-evaluation, and always aim to make your next All-Age Service even better.

The key question in evaluation is: 'was the Big Idea central throughout?' because that is a way to ask if we kept the Bible as the main thing. Be kind, but be ruthless. Identify areas to develop or avoid in subsequent services. Lovingly push one another to think about how to plan things better to keep the Big Idea at the heart of the service.

You may feel that, yes, the service was thoroughly biblical throughout and every element was shaped by the Big Idea. So here's a supplementary question: 'did we <u>effectively</u> get the message across?' This gives you a chance to consider the success of the various elements of your service. Possible questions are:

- What worked well and why?
- What was it about the effective elements that made them effective?
- What didn't work and why?
- Was anything unclear or unnecessarily complicated?

Occasionally All-Age Services are a disaster! It could be that the Big Idea wasn't clear. Maybe the Big Image was not an effective vehicle for the message. Possibly it was just 'too big' and so distracted rather than helped. Did anything compete with, distract from, overwhelm, or drown out the 'word'? There may have been too many elements which led to a lack of clarity. Perhaps the talk simply missed the mark.

Some services will be great, and you'll be praising God that it all came together superbly. Others will not be so good, and you'll be praising God that 'in all things <u>he</u> works for the good of those who love him,' (Rom. 8:28) despite, and even through our failures! It happens, so learn from your mistakes and move on to the next service.

Here's one further review question to ask: 'was there a chance for everyone to engage?' It may be the case that whole sections of the church family were not catered for. Perhaps it was too weighted towards adults and so the children switched off. At other times, it might have been weighted too much towards the children and the adults settled into spectator mode rather than engaging. Don't assume that all children and all adults engage with activities in the same way. For example, my son (a child) doesn't enjoy actions songs or getting messy but my wife (an adult!) does.

And it may be that an individual simply doesn't like All-Age Services. (If that's the case, point them to the first chapter in this book!) Maybe temperamentally, they're happiest to be on the edge of this style of service. But sometimes a lack of engagement in an All-Age Service can reflect a deeper spiritual malaise. An observant church leader might follow up individuals and privately pastor them, if appropriate.

Summing up

We want the whole church to grow together. We are persuaded that All-Age Services are a brilliant opportunity for this. In those services (as with every service), the key thing is that the Bible needs to be faithfully taught.

That is why we begin by working hard on the Bible passage until we have a clear Big Idea.

Then, collaborating with others, we pursue a Big Image to best get across this Big Idea. Using these, we then plan all the elements of the service around what God is saying in His Word.

At every stage of planning and doing an All-Age Service, the Bible is in the driving seat. We are encouraging every person present to engage with God in His Word. Because as they do, God builds His church.

4
WORKED EXAMPLES

Here come nearly thirty worked examples of All-Age Services that we have been involved in. They model the approach this book has been describing.

For many churches with a monthly All-Age Service, you may already be rubbing your hands with glee, thinking that this sounds like three years' worth of short-cuts. You may even have jumped straight into reading the book here, in which case: welcome. (You do know books don't normally start in the middle, don't you?)

But! ... You can't use our book quite like that. It is deliberately not 'plug-and-play'. We haven't given you everything you need. You will still need to do your own work. Certainly you will need to do a lot more studying the Bible passage. You need to be clear why you choose to do everything you will do. You need to work it out for your own situation (where there's a huge fifteenth-century stone font at the front, or where there's only two children in the 7–11 age bracket).

What you have got is an ideas board. You might think that some ideas are just plain silly. Leave them on one side. Some of our ideas might spark off other ideas that are much better. Good! For some, the Big Image is SO big, and so dominates the talk, that the rest of the service should be more 'standard'. For others, there is a smorgasbord of endless possibilities, so don't try to include everything! (And we would just ask the Johnny-come-latelys to read chapters 1 to 3. That will make these examples much more useful to you.)

Some of the ideas in these examples will be very stretching. You might think they require massive staff teams, hordes of volunteers, weeks to prepare, and a big budget. In reality, we had none of those things! All the ideas here have been tried in normal small-to-medium sized churches with modest resources. Don't be daunted. Whilst we would challenge you to attempt something more ambitious, if any of the specifics seem beyond you, feel free to scale them down. Adjust what is impractical, discard what is unpalatable and modify what is helpful.

But whatever you do, let's get preaching at All-Age Services!

GENESIS 4:1-16

Thinking about the passage

After the Fall, things get worse. God warns Cain about the temptation to sin but Cain rebelliously continues. So sin grows and we have the first death. <u>And</u> it's a murder. <u>And</u> it's fratricide. <u>And</u> it wipes out a quarter of the world's population. The blood cries out for justice: of course, such scandalous sin must be punished.

But there is also God's kindness in this chapter: He protects Cain, and gives more children to Adam and Eve, which in turn points us forward to the coming of Jesus. There's a link here to Hebrews 12:24 and the blood of Jesus that speaks a better word: His blood cries out that sin has been punished (and we are forgiven because of His death).

THE BIG IDEA

Sin gets worse and must be punished, but God is also still gracious.

Exploring the imagery

Murder. A crime of passion. Bloodshed and violence. Perfect stuff for an All-Age Service!

THE BIG IMAGE

A crime scene investigation of a murder.

Ideas Board

- When people entered church, they were entering a crime scene! They had to duck under the hazard tape and have their fingerprints taken by 'the police'. There was an outline of a body taped out on the floor in the middle, with a tomato ketchup bloodstain by its head. There were also numbered crime scene markers scattered around, and security lights to floodlight the crime scene.

- The Bible reading (Genesis 4:1-16) was performed as a 'police reconstruction'. It was mimed out as somebody did the reading.

- We then had a quiz to see if people were listening well to the reading, i.e. being a good detective! We split the congregation into small teams and had them put their hands up to answer questions. However, we planted people in one of the teams and had them cheat. The quizmaster kept choosing 'the cheat', even though they shouted out / conferred / got it wrong, etc. We also planted someone in one of the other teams to stir up dissent about this awful cheating. By the end, everybody was literally 'crying out' for justice! We were able to make the link to the way that Abel's blood also cried out for something to be done about it.

- I acted as a Detective Inspector, interviewing Adam and Eve, across a police room table, as parents of the victim, to give us some background on the conflict. This effectively covered the teaching of verses 1-5.

- Then I interviewed the suspect Cain. ('Formal interview regarding the murder of Abel Mann. Please state your full name and address for the benefit of the tape ...' 'I don't know anything about it, officer. I'm not my brother's keeper, for goodness' sake!') This covered the internal struggle of verses 5-9.

- Image of Cluedo. Who dunnit? It was 'Cain ... east of the garden ... with a rock'. Only one person in the police line-up.

- Link in the sermon to 'blood which talks'. The blood on the church floor cried out for an explanation! Abel's blood cried out 'Punish!' Jesus' blood cries out 'Punished' because He died for us.

GENESIS 6–9 (Noah)

Thinking about the passage

This well-known children's favourite is, of course, horrific: the entire world population (bar eight) is 'missing presumed dead'. God's intention was that the world should be 'filled' with 'missionary-gardeners' who extend the borders of Eden, but instead it is 'filled with violence' (Gen. 6:11, 13). And His just verdict is to blot out what He has made (6:7), and, in an act of de-creation, He joins up the separated waters of Genesis 1:6-7 (waters under, waters above) as water comes, in 7:11, from below and above.

The story is also constructed around the central turning point that 'God remembered Noah' (8:1). In the midst of His judgement, God saves. What must I do to be saved? Get on board the lifeboat! Eight people do so, and are 'brought safely through water' (1 Pet. 3:20). This small group of the godly huddled together, safe from God's judgement outside, is like a picture of the church. This story gives us confidence that God will bring Christians safely through the fire of the day of judgement (2 Pet. 3:5-7).

THE BIG IDEA

God rescues from God's own judgement.

Exploring the imagery

It is difficult to make the tone of the talk/service match the tone of such a dark passage. It must be sombre. And yet. It is also an uplifting story of a wonderful salvation. In working out how to tell this story, we focussed on 'safety' and 'rain' ... which led us to umbrellas! Many churches collect lost property umbrellas, and here's a way to make them useful again (– we used about 30 in this service!).

THE BIG IMAGE

Umbrella ... it provides safety from rain.

> ## Ideas Board
>
> - This service was part of a sermon series going through Genesis 1-11. It built on ideas that had been explained to adults in previous weeks (the nature and extent of sin, death as the pronounced judgement, etc).
>
> - Telling a story with multiple usage of a single prop is hard. The talk required lots of practice, but the effect of a stage full of opened umbrellas was 'magical' and, somehow, surprisingly moving. I swiftly retold Genesis 3-5 using lots of grey and black umbrellas to represent the build-up of 'things going wrong'/sin ... and then rain clouds (= God's judgement). Blue was 'sea'. (A fish or animal umbrella for those drowned?) We also had a tartan umbrella, and so told the story of one 'Fraser McNoah' (a storyteller with a Scottish accent!), and that umbrella then also became 'the ark' (upturned like a boat). A yellow umbrella was the sun, and white (opening and shutting) for the flying dove. Rainbow umbrella too, obviously! Etc. We pre-recorded sound effects (e.g. rain, thunder, wind-and-rain, birdsong, etc.) which accompanied the storytelling. The main point: God provides a place to be safe from His judgement. Application: be safe!
>
> - Give thought about how to confess sin in this service. The story tells us that God must and will punish sin,

so confession should be done deliberately and thoughtfully, not merely *de rigueur*. For example ... sins could be written down and burnt, or sins that make dirty are washed away, or a whiteboard could be rubbed clean. Or, alternatively, use a Sharpie indelible pen (on a T-shirt?) so that writing cannot easily be removed, etc.

Are there additional ways to use umbrellas elsewhere in the service (without confusing the 'metaphor')? For example, this service could be done in the open air. You could play 'pass the umbrella' and when the music stops everyone gets sprayed with water pistols except those under the umbrella.

GENESIS 12:1-9

Thinking about the passage

This could properly be described as the pivotal passage in the Old Testament where God sets out His plans for His people in the form of promises He makes to Abraham. These promises are how Eden will ultimately be restored, and they point us to the work of Christ. Galatians 3:8 describes these promises as 'the gospel announced in advance'!

This passage also introduces Abram to us. The human story of leaving his homeland shouldn't be ignored by focusing solely on the theological content of the promises. Abram puts his faith in God: this raises the question 'is He worth trusting?' If God fails to keep these promises, then we can rightly call His trustworthiness into question.

The rest of Genesis (and indeed the rest of the Bible) is about how God can be trusted, how these promises are worked out.

THE BIG IDEA

God's Promises to undo the effects of sin can be trusted.

Exploring the imagery

Whilst the promises are the most important aspect of this passage, the response of Abram to the God who makes the promises can help us to connect with them. Can he trust God? Why does he trust God? Why do we trust God?

THE BIG IMAGE

Trusting promises.

Ideas Board

- We taught this passage at an All-Age Service as part of a series on Genesis. In fact, we had already had a 'normal' sermon on this passage a few weeks earlier but wanted to revisit it with the whole church family as it is so foundational to our understanding of faith. We used Genesis 24 as an illustration of Abram's trust in the promises and then went back to Genesis 12 in the talk to teach about how we can trust God.

- We retold Genesis 24 using a camel puppet talking about what they had seen. The Service Leader interviewed the Camel to draw out the salient content from the chapter. We emphasised how what had happened in that chapter was an example of Abram trusting in the promises God had made to him.

- Trust exercises were used by the Service Leader (the kind of thing where someone falls back into the arms of someone else) to show how we can trust someone else who promises they will catch us. We arranged for the third person to be 'dropped' (onto a hidden crashmat you'll be pleased to know) after which point no one trusted the Service Leader to catch them.

- For a time of confession, we got people to think about promises they had failed to keep (giving examples appropriate to different age groups) and then asked for God's forgiveness and for help to be true to our word. 'And thank you that you are <u>not</u> like us. You always keep your promises. So we can trust that you will keep your promise to forgive us ...'

- Before the talk we had another sketch with a different puppet (though you could do it with two real people!) in which the puppet had been let down by a broken promise and was unsure how she could trust her Grandad's promise to take her for pizza. She is reminded how her Grandad has always kept his promises in the past.

- The talk looked back at the promises made to Abram and how God had already begun to fulfil them in Abram's life. I had various planks of wood with promises written on them and laid the planks in a gap to stand in them to see whether they could be trusted. (We had carefully cut the ones with unkept promises so that they would break when stood upon). Only the ones with the promises from Genesis 12 held my weight. As I stood on each of the planks, I explained how the promise is fulfilled in Jesus.

JOSHUA 3–5

Thinking about the passage

Joshua is all about the land: crossing into the land (chs. 1–5), taking the land (6–11), dividing the land (13–22) and keeping the land (23-24). And 'the land' is significant because of the promises to Abraham in Genesis 12:1-7. God's solution to the 'curse' of Genesis 3:14-19 (which we see worked out in the dark stories of chapters 4–11) is a promise of 'blessing' for God's people who will be brought to the place of His blessing. This book of Joshua is the point in the Big Bible Story where 'not one word of all the good promises that the Lord had made to the house of Israel had failed: all came to pass' (21:43-45). Against all the odds, He has brought His people of promise to the land of promise. It's happened. God has done it!

So this entry into the land is very poignant. And the fact that their arrival there is all God's doing is something worth remembering forever!

THE BIG IDEA

Always remember!

(Full version: Always remember that God dried up the water to bring His people home.)

Exploring the imagery

This is early in a series of sermons in Joshua. There is a lot of story to tell ... so we gave time to that: never underestimate the power of a well-told story!

These chapters are all about crossing the Jordan (the word 'to cross' comes 22 times in chapters 3–4). But how impossible it is to enter into God's promises: just consider the depth of the water (3:15)! Three incidents in these chapters are about

emembering: stones (4:1-7), circumcision (5:2-9) and the
assover (5:10-12). But it is the pile of 'stones' that will forever
emind Israel that it was God who did this impossible thing
4:6-7, 21-24).

HE BIG IMAGE

he pile of stones as a reminder.

Ideas Board

- I told the story on a table using lots of Duplo blocks, people and animals (– borrowing lots of bricks from various homes). Plus two identical large square tubs with water (that could easily be split apart to provide a 'dry path'). I made much of the connection back to crossing the Red Sea (when Israel originally came out of Egypt), and to the journey that had brought them all the way here. Now they are about to enter the land, as God had always promised (Duplo signpost to point the way?) ... but 'deep water' lies ahead! Obviously Duplo etc. on a table is 'small scale' (– good for smaller children who gathered around the table at the front, but hidden for most of the congregation). So, to make it visual for everyone, we projected it 'live' via a hand-held shaky camera onto the big screen ... this gave it a very contemporary, 'newsreel' feel. Curiously, it almost felt that we were all watching the actual events unfold. It was very 'fresh'.

- The storytelling can be humorous (e.g. 'there seem to be lots of penguins and seals in this river' ... and 'there's a pirate and policeman in amongst the people of

Israel' etc.), but simple and clear: multiple repetitions of the key phrase 'always remember'.

- The first talk (10 mins) was telling the story (plus 'real time' video, as described above). Later in the service, we had a second talk with three points (5 mins), with lots of reference to the Duplo 'scene': 1. Always remember God kept His promise. 2. Always remember God will keep every promise. 3. Always remember God will take His people home. How do I know? Always remember.

- Craft: make a 'remembering bracelet'. We all sat at tables and threaded twelve 'stone' beads onto a string. Just like the 'remembering pile of stones' (of Joshua 4), this was to help us 'always remember' that God keeps His promise. Everyone sat doing this craft, before and during the second talk.

- We included an item where we collected suggestions about how we remember important things: knot in a hankie, reminders on phone, making a list, photo album, wedding ring (in case we forget!), using a mnemonic, etc. You could even try teaching a simple technique for memory improvement (lots of ideas online).

ESTHER

Thinking about the passage

The story of Esther is a beautiful example of how God works quietly and invisibly through seemingly chaotic events to rescue His people. The name of God is not mentioned once in the book and yet His fingerprints are all over it, as 'coincidences' keep working together for the good of those who love Him (Rom. 8:28).

It is easy to get lost in the details, or to merely focus in on one small part of the story and miss the grand sweep of things. I was keen to help us see the details of the book but then zoom out again to appreciate the story as a whole. As such, we preached through the whole book in four sermons with the adults. Then we finished off the series with an All-Age Service, focusing on the entire book in one go. Doing it this way really brought things out for the grown-ups, and meant that the service was much richer for all the work we had done on the Bible in the preceding month.

THE BIG IDEA

God works through circumstances to raise up a rescuer for His people.

Exploring the imagery

The story is full of larger-than-life characters and events: beautiful queens, boastful kings, evil villains getting their comeuppance, brave girls risking their lives, swashbuckling battles, feasts, and weddings! It has all the makings of a good pantomime!

I was also inspired by the way many Jews celebrate the festival of Purim, which commemorates the rescue depicted in this book. Certain verses are read out in a call-and-response way. There is cheering at the exciting bits. It is accompanied with feasting. The name of Haman (boo!) is drowned out by people banging their shoes on the floor or spinning a ratchet / football rattle every time he is mentioned. Sounds like an All-Age Service to me!

THE BIG IMAGE

A pantomime.

> ## Ideas Board
>
> • This service was quite an undertaking! But well worth it. The hardest part was writing a panto script. I wrote a full rhyming script telling the story from beginning to end, including a bit of background information about the exile and the Persian Empire.
>
> • As the preacher, I was the narrator, holding the play together. The parts of King Ahasuerus/Xerxes, Mordecai, Esther and Haman were dished out to theatrically gifted members of the congregation in advance. We ran it through once before the start of the service to roughly block out our movements, but otherwise allowed it to be a bit scrappy around the edges! All the other small lines we dished out on the day. We used very minimal costumes, i.e. a crown for a king, etc.
>
> • We played the King as an arrogant idiot. (Good exegetical work went into that.) He threw sweets into the congregation in a panto style, to show generosity. But he had no power. Queen Vashti didn't come on stage when he (and the rest of the congregation)

called her! After the wedding to Esther, they stood arm in arm and we threw confetti over them. When he couldn't sleep, he sucked his thumb and cuddled a teddy bear.

- Haman was played very nastily. Lots of over-the-top evil laughs and jeering. We bought lots of whistles, noise-makers and kazoos and dished them out among the congregation. Every time his name was said, or he came on stage, we encouraged people to make as much noise as they could and shout 'boooooooo!' and 'hisssss!'

- Between various scenes, we sang songs as a congregation, much as we would have done in a normal service. Songs about trusting God during difficult parts of the story. Songs praising God during celebratory parts of the story. At the bit of the story when the Jews fast (4:15-17), we said a short confession of sin together asking God to rescue us through Jesus.

- When the decree went out about the Jews being killed, we played Chinese Whispers, passing on the message from Haman, 'I'm going to get you!' Once they'd passed on the message, people were encouraged to cry loudly ('waaa, boohoo!'). It was surprisingly moving to hear a slowly growing Mexican wave of sadness!

- In the battle scene, the congregation rolled up their service sheets and had 'sword fights' with one another! At the very end, we let off party poppers and then shared a big church lunch together.

PSALM 24:1-2

Thinking about the passage

This was the text we chose for an All-Age Harvest Service. It tells us that all creation belongs to God, including every human being because God made it all. This Psalm also asserts God's authority over His creation not simply as Creator, but also as a powerful King (vv. 7-10). To keep things simple we decided to focus on just the first two verses. In other words we knew we weren't going to say everything we could say about God's right to rule us, but we we wanted what we did say to be clear.

THE BIG IDEA

Everything belongs to God because He made it all.

Exploring the imagery

The Big Image suggests itself. As this was a Harvest Thanksgiving service we looked for ways to use usual bits of our Harvest celebration in a way which helped us teach our passage.

THE BIG IMAGE

Ownership.

Ideas Board

- We arranged the church for a traditional harvest service. We collected produce from church members during the first song, using wheelbarrows – just for the fun of it!

- We took various items from the Harvest display and then worked backwards down the supply chain to thank God for the shopkeeper where we bought it, the delivery drivers who drove it to the shop, the distribution centre workers who loaded it into the van, the workers in the factory, the farmer who grew it, and so on. All the way back to God to whom we said the biggest thank you.

- We wrote thank you notes to God for all the things and people we enjoy, which we pinned to a huge drawing of the world. We used the notes later on in the service in our prayers (and later that week in our prayer meeting).

- The service leader had a selection of photos and items and asked the church family who they belonged to (= the 'ownership' theme). You can have a lot of fun with an item like this if, for example, you ask an older church member to bring in their favourite soft toy etc. If someone has a small pet that could also be used.

- The talk made three brief (and we mean brief!) points: 1. The world belongs to God. 2. All we have belongs to God. 3. We belong to God

- Every time the service leader or preacher said, 'the Earth is the Lord's!' the rest of the church family replied, 'And everything in it!'

- We used a clip from the film Toy Story (starting at 55:45) which shows Buzz Lightyear marked with Andy's name. He thought he was a Space Ranger from the Gamma quadrant, but he was Andy's toy all along. Just as we might think we're independent and our own masters, but actually we belong to God.

- We had an Ink Stamper made which printed the words 'I belong to God'. We stamped everyone's hand at the end of the service.

ECCLESIASTES 2:1-26

Thinking about the passage

Ecclesiastes is describing what life is like in a fallen world. Whether we are godly or not, all of us share in 'the human condition'. Since Genesis 3, life is not neat: it has lots of topsy-turviness, and inexplicable loose ends. The resolution that the book promises is not a simplistic 'become a Christian and everything will have meaning'. Rather, the Preacher looks beyond this life to end-of-time judgement, for only then – in a new heaven and earth – will everything be restored.

Chapter 2 shows that in this world ('under the sun'), whatever we pursue, we cannot turn the tables. Life remains 'vanity'. That word translated 'meaningless' or 'vanity' literally means something like 'a puff of smoke': it's something we can't really get our hands on, because it is ephemeral, insubstantial, passing. Of course life in a fallen world is like that, for we were made for a better world than this.

THE BIG IDEA

You can have it all, and yet you will end up dissatisfied

Exploring the imagery

The man of Ecclesiastes 2 is chasing the best experiences that his money could buy him in this world. He reads every blog, flicks through every online review, and drools at all he sees in every shop window ...

THE BIG IMAGE

The man who had it all.

Ideas Board

- This is an unusual one! We did this (as part of a series in Ecclesiastes) for an All-Age Service on Fathers' Day. I deliberately preached to dads (explicitly asking everyone else to overhear what I was saying to them), but in an All-Age style (shorter, lots of pictures, very simple message).

- I used the image of a shop window. So I formatted all the PowerPoint slides (and there were lots!) to look like a shop window. All that we drool at ...

- One by one, in the talk, I followed through all the various things that this man used his money to try: pleasure (i.e. laughter, alcohol, foolishness [which I interpreted as celebrity], building projects, wealth and women), and then wisdom (i.e. ideas, psychology, education etc.). Is there more to life than this? I went from this to the conversation that Jesus had with the woman whose life is similarly running on empty in John 4 (cf Mike Cain: *Real Life Jesus* chapter 6).

- There are lots of resources/pictures to help make the point of this chapter, and of Ecclesiastes in general. I particularly like the banned X-Box advert 'Life is Short' (but do note that it has a 15-certificate!). But beware, multiple multimedia examples of 'what is vanity in our world' are difficult to compete with: remember (if you go to the same endpoint as I did) that we want the living water that Jesus provides to seem infinitely better than all this world affords ... not a less colourful, dull second-best!

ISAIAH 44:6-23

Thinking about the passage

Isaiah 40-55 looks ahead, from before Israel's exile until after it, to the time when the Redeemer God Himself will come to rescue His sinful people (40:3-11): do not doubt for one minute that God is able to do exactly what He says (40:12-31). How He will do that is through His servant (42:1-4), and by re-doing the Exodus (43:1-7, 14-21). He really, really will (43:8-13)!

Of course, tragically, God's people may doubt their God and look for help from elsewhere ... that might be from other nations (e.g. by forming a military alliance with Egypt) or from other gods (like the other nations do). That would be ridiculous! For the living God is the only true God. He made us and saves. There is no one like Him.

This passage is full of biting satire. 44:13-20 is meant to be hilarious. Isaiah describes a man making an idol in order to show how completely foolish it is: he bows down to a lump of wood, which is an off-cut from exactly the same tree he put on the fire. Madness! This stuff is so politically incorrect: Isaiah mocks the idolaters in a way that is the complete opposite of normal school religious education lessons (which have to tell the stories of other religions with a straight face, no matter how obviously bonkers they are).

THE BIG IDEA

There is no one like God so it is ridiculous to worship anything else.

OR (sermon slogan) A made-up thing is not the same as the real thing.

Exploring the imagery

Isaiah is trying to get us to imagine someone making an idol, so actually making something is a good way to visualise things. But, of course, we want to avoid getting people to actually make an idol (which would be somewhat against the thrust of the passage)! The concept of making something and expecting it to be real is something children can readily understand.

THE BIG IMAGE

Making something and expecting it to be real or work!

Ideas Board

- We played a game called 'What is like ...?' I showed a picture of a thing and people had to shout out things which are like that and explain why. For example, if I showed an apple, you might say an orange (they're both fruit) or an aardvark (they both begin with A). If I showed a dog, you might say it's like a table (got 4 legs) or a sweetie dropped on the floor (covered in hair). A shoe is like cheese (smelly) or an eyeball (comes in pairs). But what is like God? Nothing. He's a bit like ... erm, no. He's bigger and better than that. He is one of a kind. Link to verse 7 when God asks, 'Who is like me?'

- Everybody was given a lump of playdough. We got them to make different things and shout, 'I made this!' But the cars we made couldn't drive. The people we made couldn't walk. Imagine if we tried to make a god out of playdough. It wouldn't be real. It wouldn't hear or speak or save you. And yet, lots of people do have made-up gods.

- Later in the service, we got people to make a strong tower out of their playdough. We then got them to lean on it. It went splat. Good for nothing, unable to save or hold us up. Idols are like that. Like eating ashes (20).

- I began the talk by making a ball out of playdough: could you actually play football or basketball with it? No. A made-up thing is not the same as the real thing. I then made 'an egg'. Would you fry it, or boil it ... and then eat it? No. I made a person. I could get it to stand up, to sit down, to move around the table ... but only if I made it do those things. A made-up thing is not the same as the real thing. Can it talk? No. Can it tell me what is going to happen tomorrow? No. What if I make a little man out of my playdough, and then bow down to it and ask it to do things (I actually did each of these things, in a very exaggerated way, looking ridiculous. Make it funny in how you tell it). I did the points of the talk as 'reasons (from Isaiah 44) why God is better than a lump of wood'. 1. Because He actually exists. 2. Because He made us. 3. Because He saves us.

- Most Westerners won't be tempted by idolatry in the physical sense of worshipping an object they made. So make sure this isn't just a hard satire against other people and their silly statues. Once you have established the idea, turn the serrated language on ourselves and show up our own idolatry, which is just as crazy.

JONAH 3:1-10

Thinking about the passage

This chapter is full of turnarounds. Firstly, Jonah turns around (as promised in 2:9) and finally goes to Nineveh after having run away. His heart still doesn't seem fully in this mission but nevertheless he goes and preaches a basic message about God's impending judgement of the city (3:4).

The second turnaround is the people of Nineveh, who believe Jonah's message. Jonah had not called them to repent or told them how to respond but they do. The king of Nineveh commands everyone to 'turn from his evil way'.

The third and final turnaround is amazingly from God Himself. The king of Nineveh had hoped against hope that perhaps 'God may turn and relent and turn from his fierce anger' (3:9). Indeed that is precisely what God does in verse 10 when He relents and does not destroy Nineveh.

This links with the gospel. Jesus is like Jonah, the dead and resurrected prophet, who spent three days in the belly of the earth before coming back to call people to repentance. If we turn from our sins, God will relent from judging us for them.

THE BIG IDEA

In response to Jonah's warning, the people repent of their sin and God relents from bringing disaster.

Exploring the imagery

Jonah's literal change in direction, the Ninevites change of orientation, the Lord's change of plan, all lead us to see the focus in these verses on turning around. Not least the repetition of 'turn' in verses 9-10.

In response to Jonah's warning, the people repent of their sin and God relents from bringing disaster.

THE BIG IMAGE

Turning around.

Ideas Board

- We printed our service sheets back-to-front, with everything in the wrong order. Various bits were upside-down and required 'turning around' before they could be read. A number of sentences had the word order reversed. Other bits were written in a spiral and needed constant turning to read properly.

- I as the preacher wore my clothes backwards. They needed to turned around to face the right way again. The first two turnarounds were like that: fixing something which had been the wrong way round.

- Every time there was a turn-around in the story, I moved to the other end of the auditorium and the whole congregation had to turn their chairs around to face the new 'front'.

- You could do the hokey-cokey! After all, turning around is what it's all about!

- Jonah's short sermon was summarised as, 'You've only got one month left!' We got the congregation to chant that. Sounds very ominous with that many people saying such a scary thing!

- The King of Nineveh's proclamation was done using a megaphone. Like a public service announcement 'interrupting your usual programming' to give an urgent warning. We used the image of a house on fire. If you saw a house on fire, you wouldn't simply say, 'That is interesting. You don't normally see many fires on this street.' Nor would you quietly leave the house, leaving everyone else burning inside. You would get out quickly and call others out too. This is what the king does by calling the city to repent.

- We said a confession after hearing of the Ninevites turning from sin. This had the added benefit of breaking up the talk, and making us wait with some anticipation to see if God responded graciously to their repentance. (He did. We celebrated.) The confession could involve actually turning around: stand and face the back, and then turn to face the front as we all say the words about 'turning' from our sin.

MATTHEW 13:1-23

Thinking about the passage

This is a familiar passage, but it actually presents quite a tough lesson for Christians. Jesus speaks of our response to the gospel not simply as an initial response when we first hear it, but as an ongoing response every time we hear the Word of God. The path, rocks, thorns and good soil can be seen in terms whether we accept the good news on first hearing it, with the good soil being those who are saved. However, the different types of soil also describe how we receive the truth of the gospel whenever we hear it.

We face disappointment on two levels:

- We're disappointed as we see the seed of God's Word fail to grow in people who either outrightly reject the gospel or who seem to accept it only to fall away at some later point.

- We're disappointed as we see in our own lives the times when we have failed to live as the Bible teaches us to live.

Despite those disappointments, the Word of God will always produce enormous amounts of fruit, with seeds to be sown again.

The key application from this parable is not to thank God that as a Christian you're the good soil, but to ask God to help you be good soil every time you receive the seed of His word.

THE BIG IDEA

God's harvest will disappoint us, but it won't be disappointing.

Exploring the imagery

Any gardener loves this story. As a parable it takes an everyday situation and through it teaches us spiritual truth. As a general rule the imagery in parables is so striking that it is best not to stray too far from it in an All-Age Service.

THE BIG IMAGE

Seeds.

Ideas Board

- People could be invited to bring a favourite pot plant to church with them which could be used to make the point how the seed will always grow in good soil.

- With such a good story the reading can be illustrated fairly easily by someone acting it out as it is read. It might need lots of clearing up afterwards but throwing lots of seed around the church helps to make the retelling more memorable.

- We asked a few people to share with the rest of the church family how they read the Bible at home.

- We had a recurring refrain throughout the service. Every time the service leader shouted 'Remember!', the rest of the church family shouted back 'It's what you do with seed that counts!'

- During the service we had several 'seed pictures' on the go which depicted various scenes from the Bible. These were completed after the service – there's no reason not to cut an activity short in the service if you can carry it on afterwards.

- Tables were set up around the edges which were planting stations with plant pots, water, seeds (labelled 'Biblicus Floribundi – Word of God') and soil (labelled 'good soil'). Broad beans are good to use for this as they grow easily enough at home and very quickly too. At the end of the service we provided labels to stick on the pots with the refrain printed on them along with Matthew 13:23. They also contained 'care instructions' encouraging everyone to read and listen to the Bible.

- The talk was split into two parts with the first part being a parody of a Blue Peter episode. We used the Blue Peter music and emblem and I did a Blue Peter demonstration on seed planting. I used the refrain 'Remember! It's what you do with the seed that counts!' throughout. The seeds I planted came from an oversized seed packet named 'Biblicus Floribundi – Word of God' and the word 'Bible' was written on each seed.

- After demonstrating how to plant a seed in the good soil I said 'Here's one I made earlier,' and produced a plant. This happened four times and each plant revealed related to one of the four 'soils' from the passage. The first is rock solid etc. Each seed was actually a capsule (– we used an emptied paracetamol case) and inside each was a verse from the reading relating to one of the soils. The seed case was 'found' for each type of soil and the verse read out. The final plant had lots of 'seeds' in the flower head.

- In the second part of the talk I explored the application of the passage to our whole church family.

LUKE 13:18-21

Thinking about the passage

Jesus compares the kingdom of God to a mustard seed and some yeast. In both situations, the emphasis is on it starting small but eventually growing to have a big impact.

The point is that everything to do with our Christianity may/will currently appear unimpressive. But God's kingdom will grow to fill all the earth (cf. Dan. 2:34-35): when that happens, no one will be sneering at its smallness.

THE BIG IDEA

God's kingdom starts small but will grow.

Exploring the imagery

The imagery is obvious in this passage! A plant growing from a tiny seed to a big tree. And a little bit of yeast working through the whole batch of dough. So this service aims to get people visualising the growing seed and the expanding yeast. Lots about growth and having a bigger-than-expected impact.

THE BIG IMAGE

Small things growing, especially seeds and yeast.

Ideas Board

- We did a science experiment with two clear plastic bottles containing sugar and water, adding yeast to one of them, shaking it and putting a balloon over the top of both bottles. They looked the same and the yeast was only tiny. But the yeast in one of the bottles reacted with the sugar, produced carbon dioxide, and blew up the balloon. Yeast is a small thing with a big impact.

- We held a Bake Off competition to produce a loaf of bread. One person did the recipe properly adding yeast to make it rise. The other person didn't believe that the yeast would do the job. Instead they added ridiculous things like an extra-large egg, some volumising mousse, weight gain supplements, a pair of XXL pants, a motivational poster encouraging the dough to rise ... We baked both loaves during the service and showed the results at the end. This introduced the idea that we may not believe the yeast will work, so we wrongly resort to other methods to get growth.

- I showed an ultrasound scan of our (then-as-yet-unborn) daughter: tiny at the moment but we fully expect her to grow. Jesus spoke about the kingdom of God in a similar way.

- I re-told the two stories. About the man planting a seed and how it grew. Look how small a mustard seed is. Eat some and taste what a strong flavour they have for something so small. I showed some yeast. 20 yeast cells next to each other are the width of a human hair.

Really small! But when it is hidden in the mixture, it can make bread for 100 people.

- Then I drew out the big ideas. The kingdom starts small. I got people to repeat that phrase and show with their fingers a tiny amount. I spoke about how the kingdom looks and feels very unimpressive to us.

- But thankfully it doesn't stay small. The kingdom ends big. I got people to stretch their arms wide to show a huge size. We saw how one day God's kingdom will fill the whole earth. I linked people back to the other aspects of the service to show the impact a small thing can have. Don't be fooled by how small it is, as if it can be safely ignored. Don't be ashamed by how small it is: it will grow.

- After the service, people could choose to plant some cress seeds to take away with them and see how the tiny seeds would grow into something.

LUKE 24:36-49

Thinking about the passage

Jesus has just risen from the dead, but His disciples are yet to be fully convinced. They think they are seeing a spirit. And so Jesus proves to them that He is really alive. He encourages them to see and touch Him, to help them with their doubts.

Often we stop our Easter message at that point (– 'He really is alive!'). But there is more in this story. The fact of the story leads to the message of the story. Because of His death and resurrection, repentance and forgiveness of sins are now to be preached.

The fact of Easter is the resurrection. But the message of Easter is forgiveness.

THE BIG IDEA

Jesus is alive and so forgiveness is available.

Exploring the imagery

Bit by bit, Jesus proves to His disciples that He is really alive. This is an opportunity for us to similarly show how we know anyone is alive and then apply it back into the passage.

THE BIG IMAGE

Proving that someone from the congregation is alive.

Ideas Board

- We did this on an Easter Sunday.

- I got the children to tell me the Easter story so far by feigning ignorance. 'Who is Easter all about? Jesus?! I've heard of Him. He sounds great. But what happened to Him? He got killed?! How? I bet everyone was really sad. Did they go and visit His grave? What did they see there? He was alive?! But I thought you said He died on the Friday! How could He be alive again on the Sunday? Let's look at the Bible to find out what on earth was going on ...'

- Carl Sagan said, 'Extraordinary claims require extraordinary evidence.' If these people are saying that Jesus was alive, we need to check that out. What is the evidence?

- I got a child to volunteer to come up the front and prove that they were alive. If they were alive, we'd be able to hear them. And so we got them to say something, to sing Happy Easter To You, to say 'peace to you'. And then we looked at verse 36 and saw that the disciples heard Jesus speaking.

- The disciples didn't just hear Jesus but saw Him too. So we got the child to show us their hands and feet. With our eyes closed we couldn't see them! But with our eyes open we could. Just like in verse 38 when Jesus told the disciples to look and see His hands and feet.

- We got the child to go round and give people a high-five so we could touch them and check they weren't a ghost or just a figment of our imaginations. This also had the added bonus of the child touching the congregation to prove that they were alive too! Just like in verse 38, the disciples touched Jesus.

- I gave the child a little Easter egg to eat. Just like verse 41, where Jesus ate some fish. All these things together show us that Jesus is alive. We sang songs to celebrate this.

- But the message of Easter is more than Jesus being alive. It is also that because Jesus is alive, forgiveness is available. We looked at verse 49 and the need to call everyone to repent to receive forgiveness of sins.

JOHN 1:14

Thinking about the passage

We focussed in on just one verse for a Christmas All-Age Service. The verse comes in the context of a passage all about the Word of God. The chapter begins with the nature of the word (vv. 1-4) and then responses to the word (vv. 5-13). John then describes what the Word achieves (vv. 14-18), and our verse is a wonderful summary of God's self-revelation to His world achieved by the Incarnation (not a word to use in All-Age Service without careful explanation!). It is the essence of the Christmas message – who is this baby whose birth we celebrate? That God has communicated with us means we can know Him for real. He is now 'knowable' in a way that He wasn't before Jesus came.

THE BIG IDEA

Meet Jesus: God in flesh on earth.

Exploring the imagery

Question: How can we know who God is? Answer: He reveals Himself to us in Christ.

How do you get to know someone if you can't communicate with them? You may observe them, but not really know them. We cannot get to know an unsearchable God unless He lets us get to know Him by speaking to us, to tell us what He is like.

THE BIG IMAGE

Getting to know someone.

Ideas Board

- As this was a Christmas All-Age Service we had a variety of Carols and Christmas Readings as part of the service. An All-Age Christmas Service might often be fairly traditional in style so as to not make visitors feel uncomfortable. We were careful to use accessible language throughout and maintained a fairly informal feel.

- We also included a fairly typical 'fun' retelling of the nativity story which required participation from everyone present. Each service sheet had a letter (from A to F) written in the top corner. The letters corresponded to a particular noise that those with the letter had to make at the appropriate point during the retelling. For example As were sheep who would Baaa whenever the word 'sheep' was said, Bs were angels who sang 'Hallelujah' whenever the word 'angels' was said and so on.

- The talk began with a Goldfish named Barry in a tank at the front and I tried to communicate with him. I explained how I loved and cared for my goldfish, but Barry the Goldfish didn't even seem to notice me or realise that I'm the one who provides for all his needs. I decide to try and let Barry know about me so I try speaking, then shouting, then using a megaphone, then writing a note and dropping it in and finally by putting my face in the water and speaking. I decide that the only way I can let the fish know about me is to become a Goldfish and get into the tank. The point is obvious: God became flesh.

- As I explained how God 'made His dwelling among us', I used a pop-up tent. I then spoke from inside the tent and came out and sat next to someone (prepped beforehand) to introduce Himself to them and make Himself known.

- 'Full of grace and truth'. I compared us to the ungrateful Barry the Goldfish who ignored me just as we ignore God. We showed a clip from the film Polar Express in which a naughty boy comes up on the elves' screen and they have to decide whether to give him a present or not. We're all a bit like that naughty boy and yet God graciously reveals Himself and gives us His good gifts.

JOHN 4:46-54

Thinking about the passage

This is the second sign in John's Gospel. Jesus is back in Cana and an important man has heard about Jesus being able to do miracles. He comes and asks Jesus to make a house call to heal his sick son. But Jesus doesn't go. Instead He simply says that the man's son will recover. And later in the story we discover that the boy did get better at exactly the same time Jesus said the word.

In John 20:30-31, John explains the purpose of recording all of Jesus' sign-miracles. He says that the signs are there so that we would believe something about the identity of Jesus, and that by believing we might have the life that He gives. All these aspects are present in this story. We have a sign (the healing), we have belief (verse 50 and confirmed again in verse 53), and in response to that faith we have life (that of the boy). This miracle shows how faith in Jesus brings us life.

THE BIG IDEA

Jesus speaks and gives life to a little boy when His words are believed.

Exploring the imagery

This is a matter of life and death. Making the link between the sad sick situation and our sad sick world. If only there was somebody who could sort that out! Using medical imagery to get the idea of how much better Jesus is than any doctor. He can heal with just a word.

THE BIG IMAGE

Doctors.

Ideas Board

- This was part of a series on the miracles or 'signs' of Jesus (in John's gospel) called 'Signposts'. To introduce this idea to the children who hadn't been in the earlier sermons in this series, we did a quiz about signs. We showed road signs and people had to guess what they signified. (There are some quite amusing genuine UK road signs!) This then flagged up the idea that the miracles of Jesus were signs, pointing us to the truth about who He is.

- We played a game to introduce the idea of a medical emergency requiring treatment. The congregation huddled in small groups. Each group was given a sheet of paper with the outline of a person on it. The person had 10 areas on their body which were coloured in red like a cut or a bruise. The cuts were numbered 1 to 10. Each little group was also given a pot of plasters numbered 1 to 10. They had to take it turns to pull out a plaster and put the correct plaster on the correct wound. When they had done all 10, they had to draw a smiley face on the man and bring it up to the front. (A variation on this, for older children/teenagers, would replace the numbers of the plasters with labelled plasters like 'glossectomy' or 'arthroplasty' that have to be stuck on the appropriate bit of the body.)

- We then read a Bible story about somebody who needed to be made better, just like the person on our pictures. But they were really poorly and needed much more than a plaster ...

- I told some terrible 'Doctor, Doctor,' jokes.

- I got a child up from the congregation to dress up as a doctor with a medical kit. I then pretended to be ill and from their bag they gave me pretend tablets, but they didn't help. They put a plaster on me, but that didn't help. They pretended to give me an injection, etc. Then they pulled out of their bag ... a get well soon card! 'Is that going to make me better? Why not?' Imagine just telling somebody to 'get well' and expecting them to do it! But that's exactly what Jesus did! And the boy did get better.

- I got the children to lie down on the floor in their places and pretend to be ill. But at exactly the seventh hour ('bong, bong, bong ...') they all jumped up out of bed and bounced around. (Rewrite the words of the 'sleeping bunnies' nursery song?)

JOHN 14:1-7

Thinking about the passage

This section is a high point in John's Gospel. Everything has been building up to the death of Jesus, and this is the night before the big event. The disciples are in the upper room and Jesus has been teaching them about what is about to happen to Him. They are understandably concerned! Jesus is speaking to them to help their hearts not be so troubled (14:1) in the light of His imminent death. He is reassuring them that His death will accomplish something fantastic for them.

A destination is mentioned a number of times in the passage ('my Father's house' verse 2, 'where I am' verse 3, 'where I am going' verse 4, 'where you are going' verse 5, 'to the Father' verse 6). Jesus is going to God His Father! More than this, He is going in order to get them there as well ('I go to prepare a place for you' verse 2, 'I will come again and take you' verse 3).

As usual the disciples are a little slow on the uptake. They claim not to know the way to where Jesus is going. He makes it clear that He is the way. Indeed, He is the only way. Nobody can get to God any other way.

THE BIG IDEA

Jesus is the only way to God.

Exploring the imagery

The idea of finding your way somewhere is fairly central to this passage. So there are things you can do with directions and destinations and journeys. Or with gaining access to somewhere.

We wanted to get at the exclusivity of these claims. Jesus is the way, not just a way. No one comes to the Father but by Him.

So we wanted a central motif which underlined this exclusivity. We went with a key to get in somewhere. Only one key fits the lock.

THE BIG IMAGE

Keys.

Ideas Board

- I went to my local key cutting shop and asked them for a load of their old broken keys. I ended up getting a couple of hundred keys for about £5! Everybody was given a key when they entered church.

- At the front was a big tool box with a lock on it. (It would have been even better to have a locked door preventing entry to another room, but our building didn't provide that for us, and you need to use what you have!) I invited people up to try their keys in the lock. There were other keys scattered around the room for people to find and try. I even dumped the rest of the keys on the floor with a satisfying crash and had the kids rummage through them trying each one. How frustrating: we might never get in! Just at the last moment (taking it out my pocket and placing it on the floor: 'ooh have you tried that one?'), we found a key that did fit the lock! We opened the box to discover it was full of sweets. Call off the search! We've found the way in – hooray!

- The point we kept coming back to was that just as this key got us into the box, Jesus gets us to God. And that just as only this key got us into the box, so it is only Jesus who gets us to God. Anyone who came to me at the end could use the key to get some sweets. Anyone who didn't come or who tried to use a different key could not get any. This is not a harsh restriction but a warm invitation to come! I backed up this point by saying that, contrary to popular belief, not all phone numbers lead to me! Only one does. I gave my number to someone in the congregation and asked them to call me. (They did. I answered, saying I would call them back later!) The outrageous claim of Jesus to be the only way is not an exclusive thing, pushing people away and slamming the door, but an inclusive claim inviting people in, like me giving someone my number or the key to my house.

- To illustrate verses 2-3, I imagined Prince Charles saying that his mother's house has many rooms, showing pictures of Buckingham Palace. This is true. How amazing it would be if he said he was getting one of those rooms ready for you to stay in!

- You could play a game about finding your way somewhere and needing help. The way to God however is not a map or a Sat Nav but a person. Everybody wants to know the way. 'Can you tell me how to get, how to get to ... God?' Jesus puts up His hand and says, 'Me.'

- People took their otherwise-useless keys home with them as a reminder of what we learnt.

ACTS 1:8
(overview of book)

Thinking about the passage

Acts 1:8 is programmatic for the whole book. For Acts tells of a series of geographical steps as God's salvation plan spreads out to reach all the world, and these steps provide the structural sections for the book. The sent-Spirit gives power (chs. 1–2), so that the Word of God advanced in Jerusalem (chs. 3–7), in all Judea and Samaria (chs. 8–9), and to the ends of the earth (chapters 10–28 where the gospel reaches Rome, the centre of 'the whole world'). This advance continues what Jesus began in His earthly ministry (cf. 1:1-3), as the Spirit pushes the churches outward in new missionary activity.

THE BIG IDEA

Jesus sent the Holy Spirit so that we take the gospel to the whole world.

Exploring the imagery

Central to Acts is the spread of the gospel to the ends of the earth. And this verse sets up the story of that spread. It links gospel advance and a world map! The big application question posed is whether the word of God has yet fully advanced to the ends of the earth ... has everyone everywhere yet heard the gospel?

We used this for a 'World Mission Sunday'.

THE BIG IMAGE

A world map, to show the spread of world population (in terms of chairs!)

Ideas Board

- I wanted to show the spread of the gospel around the world. So I cleared away all the chairs in our meeting room/church to 'draw' a world map that fills all the available floor space. To do this: print off an A4 scale map of the world, and superimpose a grid over the top it. Divide your floor area into a grid of the same proportions as the map. Using your printed map, plot out a world map, using bright coloured, wide masking tape to draw landmass areas on the floor, filling your church.

- Then I set out chairs for our Sunday meeting on that map, with chairs representing population. I used a website to find population totals for significant geographical areas (e.g. Africa, India, South America, Europe, Australasia, etc.). And with some simple maths, I calculated how many chairs in our normal Sunday arrangement should go into each landmass to represent population concentration (for example, India and China were very crowded, Europe had only one chair in it). When people arrived for church, this looked bizarre (– for example, there was a lot of space where 'the oceans' are), but when people later realised what the seating plan represented, it was a very striking moment. You might like to include a mini 'world geography' or 'world population' quiz early on in the service.

- We used large signs (on microphone stands) to mark the places where our mission partners were. Get information from the mission agencies that your church supports (e.g. ask to borrow display stands), and up-to-date news from mission partners. We displayed these at the back of church and printed off info for people to take home and use in the prayer time. We've also held a church lunch serving food from these different parts of the world.

- I've often included a live Skype interview with our mission partner(s): this is a superb way to make them feel 'close'. We projected their 'speaking head' onto the screen. If you do this, don't forget to pray with them 'live'.

- We used information from 'Operation World' and found out information about 'unreached people groups' (from joshuaproject.net). You might use this info to show how many Christians there are in different parts of the world (perhaps the proportionate number of red hats to be worn in each area of the world). In our prayer time, we moved around the map to pray for Christian work in different regions (especially noting our connections in each continent).

- Link this topic to our local evangelism: it's 'Jerusalem' as well as 'the ends of the earth'. We've used prayer cards (i.e. everyone to 'list the names of three friends you are praying that the gospel will reach').

ACTS 10:1-48

Thinking about the passage

In the book of Acts, the gospel has been going out beyond the confines of Judaism (see Acts 1 above) and in this chapter, the gospel first moves out 'to the ends of the earth'. So, the apostle Peter shows that this gospel really is 'international', as Cornelius (a Gentile, if ever there was one) is converted.

The focus of the service was Peter's vision (vv. 9-23), but that can only be understood in relation to what God is doing in the life of Cornelius. In fact, verse 28 is the key to understanding the vision: nobody is beyond the reach of the gospel.

This marks a huge shift in thinking for Peter – he thought there were strict rules about the extent of God's grace but the Lord graciously shows him otherwise.

Keeping things simple, we followed two lines of application:

- God's acceptance of us is not based on the rules we keep.

- God welcomes anyone into His Kingdom – not only people just like us.

THE BIG IDEA

God welcomes anyone – it's not about the rules.

Exploring the imagery

God uses food to make His point to Peter. This is such a strong image in the passage – too strong to ignore! – so we decided to play with it. We wanted to show how Peter was convinced to change his perspective in a way that would help to shape our own understanding. There are some pretty unsavoury foods hinted at in the passage and it made us think of the weird concoctions of an experimental chef ...

THE BIG IMAGE

A Bistro Café.

Ideas Board

- We set the church up like a French Bistro Café and called it 'Chez Pierre'. It was a café-style service (i.e. around tables) but it would have worked too in a more formal set-up. The theme from 'Allo, Allo' was playing as people came in and some of the Youth Group were dressed as waiters and waitresses serving coffee and croissants to people as they sat down. The Service Leader was the head waiter.

- As we wanted to hear the whole story of Peter and Cornelius we split the chapter into 3 parts (roughly in line with the NIV headings) and asked each table to divide into pairs to read one part and then tell the rest of the table what happened in their bit.

- I played the part of Peter and the talk took the form of an extended sketch, with Peter visiting the restaurant and interacting with the Head Waiter. Throughout the 'talk' the following two responses were used: God won't accept me if I eat x ... IT'S NOT ABOUT THE RULES, and God doesn't like people like that ... GOD WELCOMES ANYONE.

- The waiter brings Peter various plates of food which Peter rejects with the first response above. We had fun with the various foods we offered: Snake Surprise (which made Peter fall off his chair), Camel Casserole (which gave Peter the hump, with a variety of other camel jokes thrown in for good measure), Badger

Burger (from the 'sett' menu), and Chameleon Coffee (which kept changing colour) with After Eight 'Minks'. At the end, Peter seems to hear the voice of the congregation and wonders if God is trying to tell him something.

- Peter then gets interrupted by a variety of people inviting him to a party (we used a variety of modes of communication, including carrier pigeon – not a real one! – by which he received the invitations). The invitations came from a series of 'undesirables' – Naughty Nick, Lying Laura, Murderous Mike etc. Each one was rejected with the second response above. Finally 'Normal Nancy' turns up at the door and the waiter acts as a messenger between her and Peter, who asks if she's a Jew. She isn't, so he rejects her invitation too.

- Peter finally puts two and two together and realises what God has been telling him. The waiter then questions Peter to highlight the teaching points.

- We continued to push the application in our prayers, confessing that we have been like Peter, and praying specifically for a particular person we knew who we thought was 'least likely' to turn to Christ.

ROMANS 1:18-25

Thinking about the passage

Romans 1:18-32 is the start of a section that ends at 3:20. 'Paul is about to expound a wonderful salvation. But first, he establishes the need for it by showing that all people are sinful' (Morris).

There is a problem that means we need salvation, and this problem starts in man's thinking: everyone knows that God is there and that God is God, but everyone believes the lie that God can safely be ignored. God is angry with mankind for this rebellion and, in His anger, gives him up to his own sin. 'To enjoy forever the horrible freedom they have demanded' (C. S. Lewis). Our threefold 'exchange' (vv. 23, 25, 26) is matched by God's threefold 'gave them up' (vv. 24, 26, 28). Note then that our wrong behaviour is the result (and not just the cause) of God's anger.

The chain is:

sin –> wrath –> sins.

The chilling end (v. 32) is that mankind not only continues down a path which is clearly signposted 'death', but encourages others do the same.

THE BIG IDEA

God is angry because we have rejected Him.

Exploring the imagery

When humankind consistently rejects Him, God doesn't immediately bring on us the final judgement of irreversible destruction that we deserve. Instead, His anger is shown by 'handing us over' to that awful 'without-God-world' that we've declared we want. Our 'unilateral declaration of independence' has reaped a whirlwind.

THE BIG IMAGE

Choosing to live life in a rubbish bin.

Ideas Board

- This talk is known as 'The One with the Wheelie Bin'! Health and Safety would have a field day with this ... as became painfully obvious when we tried it!

- We played Louis Armstrong's 'What a wonderful world' as people were arriving into church.

- We began the service with 'noisy praise'! We divided the congregation into animal groups (e.g. sheep, cows, monkeys, lions, etc.). When their animal was called, they made a huge noise: 'the xxx all praise the Lord'. And everyone else replies: 'Let them all praise the name of the Lord!' All creation declares how wonderful God is!

- For the talk, I told the story of 'the wheelie bin men'. 'Once upon a time ...'. I described a brilliant world that God made: look at the big things He made (e.g. mountain, whale, sea) and the small (e.g. my eye, or my thumb [cf 'in the absence of any other proof, the thumb alone would convince me of God's existence' Isaac Newton]). Obviously everyone knows God made it all: God has made that very obvious! But some people, although they knew God, decided that if God could run this world, then why couldn't they? They'd decide what is best and how things should be. They started to think that life in a wheelie bin looked good (– it's cosy and warm and safe) ... we don't need God, they said, we can choose to live wherever we want to (climbing into the bin). And we can decide whatever we want to do in our bin. In fact (shutting the lid of the bin – you'll need a microphone) it's much better in here. What God? There's no God in our world! I know it's dark in here, but you can still feel what we've got in here ... lovely smelly vegetables and thrown away, mouldy pizza scraps ... it's all so lovely and squidgy and wet ... so much rubbish cardboard too ... mmm this is fun ... and we can get as dirty and messy as we like, and no one tells us off. They started to think that dirt was clean, and bad was good. Then opening the lid of the bin to sit on the edge (NB this is when the bin fell over ... unintentionally! And to my cost!): what do you think God did? Of course, He was very frustrated, and angry, and sad (because the life of the wheelie bin men was very pathetic). He could have just tipped the wheelie bin men out of their bin by force. But He decided to let them carry on living in there, hoping they'd discover the awfulness of the choice they'd made. God gave them up to their new wheelie bin world. He sent them messages. Lots of them. He watched and waited. Until ...

- You could now fast-forward all the way to Judgement Day. Or to Jesus deciding to come into the wheelie bin to show the way out ... etc.

ROMANS 3:21-26

Thinking about the passage

Paul has been writing a devastating critique of humanity and the danger we all face before a holy and just God. He speaks of God's anger being poured out against all ungodliness (1:18-32) before explaining that all people (Jew and Gentile alike) will rightly be judged according to what they have done (2:6). In chapter 3 Paul defends the justice of God in condemning His chosen people (1-8) and demonstrates that nobody has any claim to be in the right with God (9-20).

The prognosis is very bleak indeed. All sinners – everyone, everywhere – justly face the wrath of God. How can a holy God possibly declare anybody in the right with Him if everything Paul has written before is true? That is the good news of the gospel that Paul now begins to expound. This passage begins with what has to be one of the most welcome 'But nows' in the Bible.

The answer to the universal problem of sin and judgement is Jesus (which was always God's plan). Paul reiterates just how in the wrong we are (23) before showing that by grace God makes us right with Him (24). He then explains how God is able to act justly in this because of the substitutionary death of Christ (25-26).

THE BIG IDEA

God is right when He says those in Christ are right, even though they are wrong.

(This Theme Sentence actually comes from Australian evangelist, John Chapman. It's brilliant!)

Exploring the imagery

Given the context of our passage, we wanted to explore things that seem wrong but are right. The images of ticks and crosses were a major feature in our service.

THE BIG IMAGE

Right & Wrong.

Ideas Board

- We set the church up 'all wrong'. You are obviously constrained by your church building, but do what you can to make people think 'This is all wrong!' as they walk in. We turned the usual set-up round by ninety degrees and put the chairs out at a 'jaunty' angle. We also gave out badly folded service sheets and the writing on the front was full of mistakes.

- After the first song everyone was invited to make a 'prop' that would then be used in the rest of the service. The prop was a simple construction made of seven pieces of rectangular card joined at the ends with split-pins (in a straight line) that could be folded into a cross (X), a tick (✓) and a cross (✝). (Try it, then this makes sense!) I had a giant one to use at the front.

- We got our usual 'victim' up to the front. He was dressed in a dustbin liner and had a rubber glove pulled over his hair. I made him stand on a tarpaulin. I then retrieved a previously hidden custard pie and asked the congregation if they thought I was going to 'custard-pie' him (they showed their answer with the cross or tick). I then invited our most unassuming church family member to the front. I said "I have one custard pie. Who am I going to use it on? Does anyone want to change their answer?" I then 'custard-pied' the elderly saint who had joined me at the front. I made the point that everyone thought they were right but in fact they were wrong! (Needless to say I had had the necessary conversation with the pie recipient beforehand!)

- We watched a video that showed a girl pushing her brother off his bike and then discovered that she did this to protect her brother. What seemed wrong was in fact right!

- For the talk I picked up on the previous 'item' and said we're all much more wrong than we could possibly imagine because we are all wrong with God. What can we do about it? We thought about how we pretend we're right, Tippex out the wrong, compare ourselves to others, highlight the 'right stuff' or blame others.

- We then used our props to show that wrong can be changed to right. If something is wrong, how do we make it right? We add more salt to soup or cut some length off a pair of trousers (I did both) – but God doesn't change us to make us right. He does something Himself to change our problem and declares us to be right.

- How does this work? How is He right to do this? If He changed us to make us always right (the tick) and never wrong (the cross) we'd be OK with that. It would be like refolding our service sheets properly or rearranging the chairs back to their proper place, but we're more like the front of the service sheet – we're all wrong and can't be changed. God declares us right and He is right to do this because Jesus takes our wrong and gives us His right on the cross – we all used our prop to visually demonstrate this.

ROMANS 8:28-30

Thinking about the passage

Romans 8:28 is regularly misapplied to mean something like 'everything will work out well for you'. It is true that the context in Romans 8 is about our Christian experience in this fallen world, where we 'groan' and 'hope for what we do not see' (vv. 18-25). And in that 'suffering' experience, we can have confidence that God will be working in everything to make us more like Jesus. And He will certainly complete what He's started: He will glorify those He foreknew, predestined, called and justified. So the 'good' (in verse 28) is glory then, not relief now.

Now, look again at our verses. The twist in the passage is that God's ultimate purpose ('in order that') is to exalt Jesus as 'firstborn among many brothers' so He is preeminent in a large family. It takes a Copernican revolution to see that God's purpose is not all about me, but all about Him.

THE BIG IDEA

God is at work through all the ups and downs of life: He will bring us to glory, and exalt Jesus.

Exploring the imagery

There is a contrast here. We see our life here as a series of ups and downs. God sees our life here as a canvas on which He is tracing out His purpose. His purpose can be seen in two ways: He is working in 'all things' to make us like Jesus, and He is working in 'all things' to exalt Jesus.

Life is (to us) like a game of snakes and ladders. God's perspective is like a different dimension – a literal ladder set up on the board. And at the top of the ladder is not us (as we might like) but the Lord Jesus.

THE BIG IMAGE

Snakes and Ladders board (plus additional step-ladder).

Ideas Board

- The Planning Group co-opted a few volunteers to make a huge Snakes and Ladders board (roughly 7m square) painted in very bright colours. We put it in the middle of our church meeting space with everyone (unusually) sitting on all four sides (i.e. church 'in the round').

- For one activity, we gave everyone Post-it notes, and asked them to write down good things which happen (and then come and stick them at the foot of the 'ladders' on the Snakes and Ladders board). And also, to write down bad things (and put them at the top of 'snakes').

- We prayed for one another in the ups and downs of life, using the written down good things/bad things as the basis for prayers. The person leading the prayers gave thanks for the ladders, and asked for help with the snakes.

- You could also use the board and play the game (for a quiz?), using an oversized dice. (Online, you can buy a 16cm cube foam dice, or double-sized inflatable dice.)

- We had a 'Copernicus sketch'. A 'mad scientist' (– a bit like TV presenter Johnny Ball: look him up!) demonstrated his theory that the earth is not the centre of the universe.

- During the talk, I walked on the board, using the snakes and ladders to make the point about life's 'ups and downs'. And then I climbed a real ladder, set up in the middle of the board, to make the point about God seeing the whole thing from a different angle.

- Onto each of the five steps of the ladder, I hung large labels with the words 'foreknew', 'predestined', etc. In all life's 'ups and downs', God is working in the Christian to ..., and eventually to get us to the top. Actually the ladder isn't about simply getting me to the top. At the top is Jesus, exalted as 'the firstborn among many brothers'. God's purpose is about making us more like Him. (I referred back to the Copernicus sketch: I need to see that I am not the centre of the universe, either!)

- Then we upturned the prayer time after the talk, so that now we thanked God for 'all things' – snakes and ladders alike. Every one of them is part of God's plan. And we included a confession about not trusting God's providence in 'all things'.

- The final song was all about an exalted Lord Jesus. God's plans are all about Him and not all about us.

1 CORINTHIANS 12:1-7

Thinking about the passage

In this section of his letter, Paul is writing to the Corinthians about what they should be doing when they come together as a church, and in these verses he sets out some general principles about spiritual gifts.

In verses 2-3, he speaks of the common spiritual experience of all Christians: there's no hierarchy of spirituality. All spiritual gifts are of equal value. You're not worth more to God if you have a certain gift. Declaring truthfully that 'Jesus is Lord' is the only marker of spirituality that counts.

In the next verses (vv. 4-6), Paul shows how spiritual gifts all come from the same source: God gives them all. And if He gives them, then they are all useful, and used by God. All Christians have a gift given by God (v. 7): there's no such thing as a 'giftless' Christian. And the gifts are given for the common good. In other words, they all have the same purpose – to build up His church.

Paul is flattening any attempt to elevate some Christians above others or some gifts above others, and is underlining how every Christian plays a valuable part in the life of the church.

Probably for a 'normal' sermon we would have finished the section at verse 11, but in order to make the section manageable for an All-Age Service we thought the first seven verses were sufficient.

THE BIG IDEA

We all have a gift from the same giver, of the same value, for the same purpose.

Exploring the imagery

This passage exposes how bad it is when we make comparisons about our relative usefulness in our church family. The idea of 'gifts' led us to a Big Image of 'presents'. We thought about how we judge the worth and usefulness of presents we receive.

THE BIG IMAGE

Presents.

Ideas Board

- Although this service was in February, we set up a 'Christmas Scene' at the front of church. Around the Christmas tree, there was a huge pile of presents of varying size and differing quality of wrapping.

- Initially we used the presents to make the opposite point of the passage. I searched for a present for me under the tree but there wasn't one – we didn't all have a gift. Then, two primed people came up to get their presents: one had an enormous, beautifully wrapped gift and was delighted and proud, the other found their tiny, badly wrapped present and was disappointed and jealous. Then, two identical presents were given out to two different people. When they opened them, they both contained chocolates: one person greedily scoffed the lot, and the other shared theirs with the church family. The gifts weren't used for the same purpose.

- We had a basket of identically sized boxes, enough to give one to everybody at church, (we needed to recruit some keen 'wrappers' to prepare for this service!)

They were wrapped in a variety of different colours. The idea was that there were different gifts but all were equal in value. Each gift was labelled 'With love from God'. These were given out so that everyone had a gift from the same giver. Inside each box was a copy of the Bible passage and a handwritten note which said 'You have my gift, now build my church.' I used these presents throughout the talk to help illustrate the Big Idea.

- As we thought about all gifts from God being of the same value, I handed out a sheet of paper which listed various 'jobs' within the church and asked people to grade them from one to ten in order of importance in thirty seconds. We then screwed up our pieces of paper and threw them in a bin at the front because they represented completely unbiblical thinking. I then had a powerpoint slide showing all the 'jobs' within the church, and every one was graded with a score of ten.

- During the final part of the talk, lots of people worked together to build 'a building' from the presents under the tree: we were working together with one purpose. Actually, the building turned out to be very shaky, so people had to stand around it, supporting it ... of course, this only served to reinforce the point!

- We also played with the idea of baking a cake together as a church: all the ingredients are equally needed, and combine for a common purpose. But we ditched this idea to keep to the single focus of gifts.

GALATIANS 5:16-26

Thinking about the passage

The Christian life is characterised by a war between the Spirit and our sinful nature: 'the desires of the flesh are against the Spirit and the desires of the Spirit are against the flesh' (v. 17). Someone 'led by the Spirit' ... that is 'every Christian', not 'a special type of Christian' (as if you could be a Christian and not be led by the Spirit) ... will 'keep in step with the Spirit' (v. 25), which means siding with Him in the battle.

THE BIG IDEA

The Christian life is a battleground so side with the winning team.

Exploring the imagery

The passage is all about a fierce battle. Or a war that's being waged. And this suggested an army theme. (This is a passage where 'the famous bit' is 'the fruit of the Spirit', but we felt that to focus on that would be to miss Paul's bigger point about the context of battle.)

THE BIG IMAGE

Army boot camp.

> ### Ideas Board
>
> • We decided that for this service the person leading and speaking should be the same as they could then be 'in character' as an Army General throughout most of the service. So, the service Leader/Preacher is wearing army fatigues, and camouflage face paint,

and the church is covered in camouflage netting, plus any other army paraphernalia you can find.

- After the first song I wandered around the church picking people up on their sloppy attire and unpolished shoes, or praising regulation haircuts and camouflage coloured clothing. This kind of thing needs to be done carefully so as to not offend anyone, but done well it can help build the family spirit of the church. Choose 'volunteers' with care and ideally inform them beforehand of the plans.

- We then had a training session to see how well people could march, which quickly and predictably (and deliberately on my part) ended in chaos. We need to walk in time if we're going to get anywhere.

- A 'Corporal' ran in with orders from HQ which she read out to the recruits. This was the passage from Galatians 5.

- My talk took the format of a training session. My first point was 'decide which side to be on'. I demonstrated the reckless self-serving of the enemy soldier, versus the loyal discipline of a good soldier.

- I explained that the battleground is the body. You could use a large military style plan (with those Second World War long sticks for moving troops around). I had a visual representation of the sinful nature moving out and the Spirit moving in. I ripped up the sinful nature and nailed it to a cross.

- Enemy spies might encourage us to peel it down from the cross and follow its orders once more, but if we keep in step with the Spirit we won't be tempted to do that as often. We tried marching again, this time with much greater success.

- The talk finished with a warning about the enemy luring us to change sides and said we need to imagine the sound of an air raid siren (which was played loudly) whenever we're tempted in that way.

EPHESIANS
(overview)

This is a bit different: it's teaching an overview of a whole book. Given the time constraints of an All-Age Service you can't hope to cover everything – but that's OK. Make sure that you've done thorough study to be very clear on the Big Idea of the entire book and commit to teaching only this.

Thinking about the passage

The 'argument' of the letter to the Ephesians is built around a number of key verses. 1:9-10 describes what God has revealed to all Christians: we know that God's ultimate plan is to bring everything together under Jesus as head. And He will achieve this for all things in heaven and in earth 'at the fullness of time'. Presumably then, the entire cosmos will be one gathering, united in recognising that Jesus has every right to be our Judge for He is the head over all.

2:11-22 tell us that God has already achieved this end point in the local church: He has brought together Jew and Gentile by the cross and united us in the church under Christ as head. He has made 'one new man in place of the two'. So, 3:10, the local church makes 'known to the rulers and authorities in the heavenly places' that God will achieve His purpose, and this is how He will do it. If He can do it for us, He can do it for all. It's a declaration to everyone and everything that God will win. The task therefore in the local church is not to achieve unity (for God must do that for us, and He has done so at the cross), but to maintain that unity (4:3): 'don't you lot mess it up'.

THE BIG IDEA

God will bring everything together under Jesus as head.

Exploring the imagery

The recurrent idea is 'two made one'. Things that are completely different are joined together/united. This is true now in the church. This will be true for absolutely everything on the last day.

THE BIG IMAGE

Large box of Lego/Duplo bricks: a complete mixture of different colours, different shapes can be joined into one thing.

Ideas Board

- This works well as an introduction to a series in Ephesians, or as a 'recap' to end a series.

- I poured out the Lego all over the floor – a complete mess. God's plan is to bring it all back together into the box. And that is exactly what He will do on the last day. So far, He has brought together ... collect a random selection back into the box, joining some together ... Christians in the church. One day, He will bring everything together ... 'sweep' all the blocks together into a heap. When God brings things together, He does it by uniting people under Jesus as head (I held a powerful torch above the bricks, pointing down to 'illuminate' everything).

- There is a lot of Lego/Duplo in church. This could be a major distraction (!), or it could be very useful. When I was using the building bricks in my talk, the younger children sat at the front (around my feet) playing with the bricks/joining them together. This made the point very well!

- I have also used a variation on this to introduce an evening for young couples to think about their marriage relationships (!), in a situation where English was not the first language. I extended the metaphor to say: 'so far, God has brought together ... collect two different colour/shape pieces, join them together ... Christian husband and wife together. And in fact lots of Christian husbands and wives in the local church. Two made one.'

- Since, doing this talk, I've thought of other ideas: During the talk, I could have two men made from Lego and then (as I was talking) combined them to make one bigger man. And/or I could have planets and stars made from Lego which I then combine to represent the cosmos being joined together.

- Beware the language about 'unity'. In Ephesians, unity is something that God achieves (not something that we have to achieve). Our job (Eph. 4:3) is to preserve the unity that He has achieved. So, I could use that one big man (that represents the church) and break it ... but then repair it to demonstrate how we need to work to maintain the unity, making sure the bricks are joined tightly.

- Another idea: I could take the head off the bigger man and convert it into a cross – Jesus is the head. (Maybe this is confusing the image ...?)

EPHESIANS 2:1-10

Thinking about the passage

There aren't many places in the New Testament where our salvation is described in the past tense, as something already completed. Here is one of them. And the image to describe such a salvation is resurrection: God made us alive even when we were dead.

Why Paul makes this point is chiefly because of the issue of 'power' in Ephesus. There is an enormous experiential gulf between the power days of Acts 19 (when an impressive ministry first brought the gospel to the city), and the normal Christian life now with its embarrassingly-imprisoned apostle and the mundaneness of workaday church life. Paul is reassuring his readers that the gospel they heard and believed was the truly powerful gospel that had indeed brought dead people to life.

THE BIG IDEA

When God saves, He brings dead people to life.

Exploring the imagery

This is one of the passages where the image is so clear and so startling that it must be allowed to drive the teaching. God is in the business of making dead people alive. This is obviously His work alone (– we couldn't hope to replicate this!), and clearly a work of undeserved, extravagant kindness.

THE BIG IMAGE

Making a dead thing alive.

Ideas Board

- The talk is all about the extraordinary change that no one other than God could possibly do. I took a frozen supermarket chicken (= something very obviously dead) and tried to make it alive. 'Some of you know that I keep chickens. I've brought one of them along with me today. But it doesn't look very well, so I'm going to try to make it better today. What could we try ...?' Things to try include ... warm it up a bit (wrap in a blanket, use a hot water bottle, and then hair dryer); try to inflate it (use a bike pump, then mouth-to-mouth); 'defibrillate' (try putting new AA batteries inside, wire it into the mains); try sewing on a new head (e.g. a dolls head); teach it to move ('walk' its legs on the ground, move its wings to get it to fly, throw across the room to 'jump start' its attempts). Lots of dialogue throughout of 'maybe it needs ... maybe I could try ... oh dear, that doesn't seem to have made it better either.' I had 'an assistant' who sat cuddling and stroking the frozen chicken between various 'attempts'. Conclude this section with lines from the Monty Python Dead Parrot sketch (e.g. 'this is an ex-chicken ...' etc.).

- 'Obviously I cannot make a dead chicken alive again. Of course not. It would take something unbelievably powerful to turn this ... into this ...' At which point, the assistant produces a live hen, and (ideally!) lets it loose to run round the building. Mayhem! This is 'The One about the Chicken' in our local church mythology: totally OTT!

- Beware: this 'image' is very powerful, so plan meticulously how you will control the image, and 'teach' clearly alongside. It almost certainly should be at the very end of the service. (Also, we learnt that some people will have 'salmonella' concerns, so perhaps use disposable gloves and/or think ahead to what you will/won't handle after touching the frozen chicken!)

- Write a confession using the idea of 'being dead in our sins'. When we ask God to forgive us, we are really asking that He will make us alive.

- Pray for evangelism, that God, in His grace, will make people alive again (i.e. save them).

PHILIPPIANS 4:4-9

Thinking about the passage

Paul's letter to the Philippians is about gospel partnership. And by that, Paul means that Christians stand firm with other Christians, shoulder to shoulder, putting self-interest aside, for the sake of others' salvation. That is what Jesus did (in the famous 'hymn' of 2:6ff): He put aside the personal comfort of living happily in heaven in order to make Himself nothing/become a servant/become a man/humble Himself to death/humble Himself to the most degrading form of death. Why? In order that others might be saved. He really did 'look not only to His own interests, but to the interests of others' (2:4). We should have that same mindset. Which is exactly what Timothy did have (2:19-22). And Epaphras too (2:25-30), when he risked his own life 'for the work of Christ'. In contrast, Euodia and Syntyche (4:2) are two women in danger of losing the plot, by failing to 'labour side-by-side in the gospel'.

It is the true, honourable, just, pure, lovely, commendable, excellent gospel that Christians need to think about (4:8-9). That's how we will make our mindset like Jesus. Allowing the truth of the gospel to deeply affect our thinking and our attitudes. In particular, Paul contrasts anxiety with prayer and rejoicing. When the truth of the gospel fills our minds and takes root in our lives, we will be able to be like Paul and rejoice in all circumstances.

THE BIG IDEA

Don't mope; rejoice. Don't panic; pray.

Exploring the imagery

There aren't immediate visual things in this passage. But the idea of worrying is something that everybody can imagine. Children know how it feels to be worried. Just as adults do too.

THE BIG IMAGE

Worrying.

Ideas Board

- At the start of the service we introduced the idea of things which make us anxious. We had a Worry-O-Meter. At one end of the room it said 'Love it'. At the other end it said 'Terrifying'. In the middle it said 'A bit nervous'. We then listed things and got people to move up and down the room to place themselves on the scale of how worried those things made them. The list included things like spiders, wasps, kittens, dentists, the dark, heights, speaking in front of people, being ill, clowns, etc.

- Everybody had a piece of paper with 'I am worried about...' printed on it. We gave some time for people to write down what made them worried. It could be the kind of thing mentioned in the previous game, or something they were going through. In the sermon, I referenced those things. And in the prayer time, we encouraged people to pray about them.

- During 'the Bible reading', we actually read out the complete opposite:

  Be grumpy in the Lord always; again I will say, mope. Let your unreasonableness be known to everyone.

The Lord is nowhere near here; do not be calm about anything, but in everything by moaning and complaining with resentment let your requests be kept to yourself. And the worries of life, which surpass all understanding, will attack your hearts and your minds. Finally, brothers, whatever is lies, whatever is shameful, whatever is unfair, whatever is dirty, whatever is horrible, whatever is offensive, if there is any badness, if there is anything worthy of criticism, think about these things. What you have learned and received and heard and seen in me – ignore these things, and the God of peace will leave you on your own.

- We then revealed that the book we had read from was not the Bible but a book called 'My Thoughts'. I explained that this is much more like how we usually behave but that the Bible told us to do the opposite. We then had the Bible reading done properly!

- You could do something about a castle. Your mind is like a castle being attacked all the time by worries and doubts and enemies and problems. But God can guard our hearts and minds, keeping us safe. (A bit like the opposite of Paul being chained up in prison with guards.)

- We sang 'Rejoice In The Lord Always' as a round. This works well as an activity too as people learn the different parts.

COLOSSIANS 3:1-11

Thinking about the passage

In Colossians, Paul is instructing Christians to continue their Christian lives as they began. They 'received Christ Jesus' as the Lord He truly is and as 1:15-20 describes Him to be. Now they must continue to 'walk in Him', this same Lord.

Chapter 3 marks a turning point in the letter. What does it mean to live with Jesus as Lord? First of all it means death to their past life so that now their present life is 'hidden with Jesus'. And since He is in heaven, they already live there too. Heaven is not just a 'future' thing, but it's brought into the present to affect life now because we are united with Jesus.

So, Paul encourages them to 'put off' what is earthly (what belongs to their past) and instead 'put on' in the present those things which belong to heaven (their future). Here's a good question to ask about any particular behaviour: is this something that I will find at the right hand of God (where Jesus is)? If it isn't, it should be left behind.

THE BIG IDEA

Jesus has given us a new past which affects the present as we live for the future.

Exploring the imagery

The main contrast in this passage is between what is appropriate for the Christian and what is inappropriate. The main image needs to reflect this contrast. The Christian is to be different because he/she has been given a new past, a new present and a new future.

THE BIG IMAGE

Incompatible neighbours.

Ideas Board

- This turned out to be one of our most ambitious All-Age Services. The Big Image was very big! At the front of church we built a row of terraced houses – a 'set' constructed from wood, with doors and windows that opened, brick facias, curtains at the windows, pot plants on the doorstep, etc. All of the houses in the row were immaculate.

- Early in the service, two puppets poked their heads through from two different houses. One of the puppets was completely out of place: they were rude, lied, got cross, and showed off about all the things they'd stolen that were now in their house etc. The other explained that since they'd moved into 'Heaven Street', their life had completely changed. They discussed what it was like living in 'Heaven Street'. The Service Leader went into the house of the 'bad' puppet (i.e. disappeared 'off stage') and we all heard comments about how smelly and dirty it was. The purpose of the sketch (at this point in the service) was to establish that the behaviour of one of the puppets was not appropriate in the street where he now lived. (The good thing about this format is that the puppet operators are hidden, and so can 'read' their script. This ensures great accuracy in the wording of every explanation. So, work hard on the script writing!)

- During the talk, I interacted with the same two puppets. The main points were: 1. We can't move into 'Heaven Street' just as we are. 2. Only Jesus can make us ready to live there. 3. Once we have an address in 'Heaven

Street,' there's an appropriate way to live: live now as if you lived there already. (NB there is lots in this analogy of 'neighbours' ... we've deliberately left lots of loose ends for you to explore, as you work hard to understand Colossians 3!)

- We had a brief quiz as part of this service in which we asked the question: what's the first thing that comes into your mind when you think of ...? The service leader filled the blank with various options, asked for answers from people in the congregation (of all ages), and revealed their own 'first thoughts' using props and images. The point of this was to get everyone thinking about what our first thoughts should be as Christians (see v2). I referred to this in the talk.

- The service sheet was given out in airmail envelopes. The Bible passage was printed out in letter style and was also in the envelopes, the idea being that it had arrived from heaven by airmail. It was read in small groups during the service.

- We taught verse 2 as a memory verse and strung it up at the front between the houses.

JAMES 1:19-27

Thinking about the passage

The Bible is so important in this passage. Verse 18 describes it as the word of truth which brought us to life. It has been implanted in our lives (v. 21). It has saved our souls (v. 21). And so (v. 20), we need to keep on receiving that word which saves us.

But 'receiving' it is not just a matter of listening. It also means actually doing what it says. We must not be like a person who sees an area where we need to change, but does nothing about it.

We are then given three examples (in vv. 26-27) of areas of life in which the Word needs to change us: words, widows, and worldliness. (This introduces the three issues that James will teach about in chapters 2, 3 and 4.)

THE BIG IDEA

Listen to God's Word and then actually do what it says.

Exploring the imagery

James is full of vivid imagery. Here the dominant image is of a man looking in the mirror but not doing anything about what he sees there. We also want to be drawing on ideas of being told to do something and not doing it.

THE BIG IMAGE

Mirrors.

Ideas Board

- We began with a game of Simon Says to see how good people were at listening. However, at the end I called up one of the adults and took them to task about how they played the game. We did a few examples up the front to make it clear that he was not doing what Simon Said to do. But he still insisted he should win the game because he was amazing at listening. But listening isn't worth much if you aren't going to do it.

- The Bible reading was printed in the service sheet 'in mirror writing'. We handed out mirrors so that people could read it properly.

- I ate a bacon sandwich and got ketchup all over my face. The children lent me one of their mirrors so I could see what I looked like. But I kept on seeing it in the mirror and then carrying on without wiping off the mess. This is what the man in the passage does. It isn't about forgetting what colour hair he has. The opposite of 'forgetting' here is 'doing'.

- We talked about the evil queen in Snow White asking, 'Mirror, mirror on the wall, who is the fairest of them all?' While the mirror said that she was, the queen was happy. But when the mirror told her she wasn't the fairest, she was furious! We can be a bit like that when the Bible shows us what we are really like, warts and all.

- After the service, the children had blank wooden mirrors to decorate and write verse 22 on the back.

JAMES 2:1-13

Thinking about the passage

James illustrates what the 'double-minded man' of 1:8 might be like with regard to other people and how he judges them. The 'double-mindedness' is seen as someone who 'holds the faith in our Lord Jesus Christ' (i.e. a Christian) and 'shows partiality' (i.e. behaves as the world). 4:4 shows why this is to two-time God.

So James gives very clear instruction about how Christians ought to be entirely impartial in their assessment of other people. If anything, priority should be given to those who would normally be least honoured because that is the pattern we have seen with our Lord. Rather than making a value judgement about other people based on their external appearance, Christians should instead exhibit the mercy we have received from God.

THE BIG IDEA

Don't show favouritism but do show mercy because that's what God has done for you!

Exploring the imagery

The imagery from the passage is about the relative wealth of individuals. We decided that a good vehicle to help us think about this image was the board game Monopoly. It can be used to think about showing mercy – to other players in your debt. It can also touch on favouritism as we vie for the best properties.

THE BIG IMAGE

Monopoly.

Ideas Board

- Just as we settled to read the passage after our first song, a church family member dressed in finery entered the church loudly. He was welcomed effusively and given a seat right at the front. As we were about to start for a second time a church member dressed in rags came in quietly. The Service Leader drew attention to him so that all turned to look at him, and then told him to stand quietly in the corner and not to disturb anyone. The passage was read with the Service Leader getting more and more uncomfortable as they read it.

- Every seat had monopoly money taped underneath it, one note per seat. Before the talk, people were asked to find the note under their seat and then we rearranged the seating so that those with the £500 notes were sitting right at the front with the £100 people behind them and so on. The £1 people had to stand at the back. Once we had established in the talk that it was wrong to show favouritism, everyone was invited back to their original seats.

- The church family was shown various pairs of pictures and asked which they preferred and why. We showed two types of food, two types of video consoles and two types of people (rich and poor). The last one was an uncomfortable question.

- Throughout the talk Monopoly references were used. For example, 'Mayfair people' and 'Old Kent Roaders' were used to refer to rich and poor (I know a minister in Mayfair who might want to use a different point of reference!). We played around with the ideas of 'Community Chest' and 'Chance' too and how you treat another player when they're in trouble. In essence Monopoly is about me winning – that is the essence of favouritism too.

- If you're feeling really adventurous you could create an enormous Monopoly board and label the board with streets from your local area ... I'd just say 'Handle with care'!

1 PETER 1:3
(Easter Day)

Thinking about the passage

The first paragraph of this letter is an instruction to 'elect exiles' to 'rejoice in your salvation'. In the context of suffering grief in all kinds of trials (vv. 6-7), Peter points them to this salvation, the outcome of their faith that they will obtain.

Christians have been born again to a wonderful living hope/ inheritance (– presumably the same thing?). This is something that is kept for us, imperishable, undefiled and unfading (v. 4), and it is something for which we are kept, by God's power (v. 5). God is keeping us for heaven, and heaven for us. Question: how can we be sure that all this is for real? Answer: the resurrection of Jesus (v. 3). For that's the point in history when our future was born: history changed and our inheritance became certain.

THE BIG IDEA

When Jesus rose from the dead, our unbelievable future was secured.

Exploring the imagery

This is a very good text text for Easter Sunday (but one that is not often used): it is not merely asserting the fact of Jesus' resurrection (which is often the subject for our Easter Day sermons), but explaining the implication of that resurrection for us (which we don't preach so often). Because of Easter, we are promised a future that utterly exceeds our current experience or even our wildest longings.

THE BIG IMAGE

What's inside an egg? ... we expect a yolk, but it's a live chicken!

Ideas Board

- The talk used the idea of new life hidden inside an egg (– eggs, of course, being a very Easter theme!). I selected a volunteer, and asked them to choose between two eggs: 'which one would you like to have cracked over your head?' Everyone expects 'egg all over his face', but, in fact, this egg was one I had previously 'blown' so was now empty: no messy situation! 'How often our hope disappoints us. But this passage says that our hope is not an empty hope, but a living hope. Let's try another egg.' I then cracked another egg, 'accidentally' dropped it onto floor, and then picked up a live tiny chick from the box by my feet. As I walked around the church cradling the tiny chick (– lots of 'aaah' noises!), I described that our future, because of Easter, is one that exceeds expectations. What God is keeping for us – as good as ever, and as good forever – is far better than we expect.

- I did consider repeating exactly the same talk the following Easter (when everyone thinks they know what's going to be inside the egg-that-exceeds-expectations). But on that occasion, when I drop the egg, I would release a live piglet rather than pick up a tiny live chick. Wow! But I never actually did this ...!

- Easter's talk of death and resurrection is particularly hard for those feeling the pain of bereavement. Acknowledging that is important (particularly because the feel of an Easter service is usually very upbeat): in the prayers, pray for 'those who find Easter hard' and repeatedly use a phrase like 'when life disappoints us'.

Group Exercise

Why not have a go as a group thinking about planning an All-Age-Service on Deuteronomy 6:1-25? We have done a bit of guiding Bible work for you. Have a look at the passage and try and come up with 'The Big Idea' and 'The Big Image' and then work your way through populating the planning sheet on the following page.

DEUTERONOMY 6:1-25

Thinking about the passage

Deuteronomy 6 is largely about a response of love to a God who loves: the great command to love God (v. 5) follows the description of who God is (v. 4). Love is the fundamental response to a God like this.

Moses sketches out what this response of love will look like in the land that God is giving His people (vv. 10-19). And he includes an example of what it won't look like (v. 16).

He then goes on to encourage God's people to remember all of God's love-in-action that they have experienced (vv. 21-25). God's people have a duty to impress this truth about God's love upon their children (verses 7 and 20) as they live out before them a life dominated by God's word to His people. Remembering daily what God is like and what He has lovingly done will mean that we will joyfully obey him as our response of love to him.

THE BIG IDEA

Exploring the imagery

THE BIG IMAGE

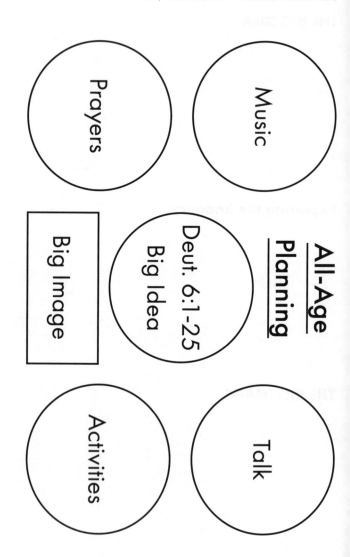

ALSO AVAILABLE IN THE GET PREACHING SERIES...

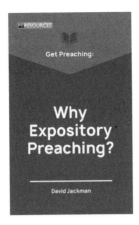

Get Preaching: Why Expository Preaching
David Jackman

- Part of the Get Preaching series
- Examines the importance of expository preaching
- Helpful suggestions for putting it into practise

At its simplest expository preaching is preaching which allows the Biblical text to direct the contents of the message, by which the church grows and flourishes.

But why is it so important?

In this short book David Jackman explains the motivation behind this method of preaching, gives instruction for putting it into practise, and works through a couple of examples of expository sermons. This book will be a crucial tool for anyone engaged in teaching God's flock.

ISBN: 978-1-5271-0385-6

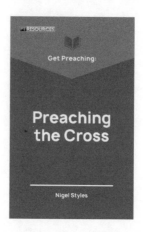

Get Preaching: Preaching the Cross
Nigel Styles

- Why it is important to preach the cross
- Helpful suggestions for putting it into practise
- Part of the Get Preaching series

The gospel is powerful; we just need to speak it.

In this very practical, short book from the Get Preaching series, Nigel Style reminds us what preaching is, what the message of the cross is, and why that is something to be heralded to all the world. Bringing these two points together he explains the importance of always preaching the cross when preaching the Bible.

ISNB: 978-1-5271-0384-9

About The Proclamation Trust

The Proclamation Trust is all about unashamedly preaching and teaching God's Word the Bible. Our firm conviction is that when God's Word is taught, God's voice is heard, and therefore our entire work is about helping people engage in this life transforming work.

We have three strands to our ministry:

Firstly we run the Cornhill Training Course which is a three year, part-time course to train people to handle and communicate God's Word rightly.

Secondly we have a wide portfolio of conferences we run to equip, enthuse and energise senior pastors, assistant pastors, students, ministry wives, women in ministry and church members in the work God has called them to. We also run the Evangelical Ministry Assembly each summer in London which is a gathering of over a thousand church leaders from across the UK and from around the world.

Thirdly we produce an array of resources, of which this book in your hand is one, to assist people in preaching, teaching and understanding the Bible.

For more information please go to www.proctrust.org.uk

Christian Focus Publications

Our mission statement —

STAYING FAITHFUL

In dependence upon God we seek to impact the world through literature faithful to His infallible Word, the Bible. Our aim is to ensure that the Lord Jesus Christ is presented as the only hope to obtain forgiveness of sin, live a useful life and look forward to heaven with Him.

Our books are published in four imprints:

CHRISTIAN
FOCUS

Popular works including biographies, commentaries, basic doctrine and Christian living.

CHRISTIAN
HERITAGE

Books representing some of the best material from the rich heritage of the church.

MENTOR

Books written at a level suitable for Bible College and seminary students, pastors, and other serious readers. The imprint includes commentaries, doctrinal studies, examination of current issues and church history.

CF4•K

Children's books for quality Bible teaching and for all age groups: Sunday school curriculum, puzzle and activity books; personal and family devotional titles, biographies and inspirational stories — because you are never too young to know Jesus!

Christian Focus Publications Ltd,
Geanies House, Fearn, Ross-shire,
IV20 1TW, Scotland, United Kingdom.
www.christianfocus.com
blog.christianfocus.com